7 Winning Strategies for Trading Forex

Real and actionable techniques
for profiting from the currency markets

Grace Cheng

HARRIMAN HOUSE LTD

3A Penns Road
Petersfield
Hampshire
GU32 2EW
GREAT BRITAIN

Tel: +44 (0)1730 233870
Fax: +44 (0)1730 233880
Email: enquiries@harriman-house.com
Website: www.harriman-house.com

First published in Great Britain in 2007 by Harriman House.

Copyright © Harriman House Ltd

The right of Grace Cheng to be identified as the author has been asserted
in accordance with the Copyright, Design and Patents Act 1988.

ISBN 1-905-461-19-2

978-1-905461-19-2

British Library Cataloguing in Publication Data
A CIP catalogue record for this book can be obtained from the British Library.

Printed and bound in Great Britain by Biddles Ltd, Kings Lynn, Norfolk.
Index by Indexing Specialists (UK) Ltd

Dedication

I dedicate this book to my husband, Pedro.

Thank you for your constant encouragement, support and love.

This book is also dedicated to my loving parents who have always believed in me.

Dedication

Contents

About The Author

Grace Cheng is an experienced, full-time forex trader who is well-versed in technical, fundamental and sentiment analysis, which she utilises in her trading. She occasionally writes for trading and investment publications such as *Technical Analysis of Stocks & Commodities*, *The Trader's Journal* and *Smart Investor*, as well as for online financial portals such as Investopedia. She has also been featured in newspapers, magazines, newsletters and on TV.

Grace is the creator of the PowerFX Course which is designed for both new and intermediate traders to jump-start their trading performance. Grace has mentored hundreds of independent traders through her PowerFX Course.

Her web site is at: www.GraceCheng.com

Preface

The global forex market, being the world's most liquid financial market, offers many exciting opportunities for traders to profit from exchange rate fluctuations. And the development of sophisticated online foreign exchange trading platforms in recent years has attracted many traders to the market – traders who seek an income in addition to their day job or those who wish to trade a new market besides stocks and futures.

Who this book is for

This book is primarily for those who are new to the world of currency trading and are curious about how they can make money from the forex market. Existing traders who are trading on demo or live accounts should also find some useful advice in this book.

Some knowledge of candlestick charting is assumed as I will be using candlesticks to display the high, low, opening and closing prices in the charts throughout the book.

Contrary to popular belief, you don't have to be rich in order to trade forex today. All you need to start is a computer with fast and stable internet access and a relatively small account with a broker.

About this book

This book describes seven fundamental and technical trading strategies for trading the foreign exchange markets. The purpose of this book is to show you how you can trade forex with these winning strategies. I will share with you some new ideas, interesting concepts, and the nuts and bolts of how you can implement each strategy more effectively.

This book is quite different from traditional technical analysis books because, while those books may document the reliability of certain technical patterns, I will explain in this book why certain technical patterns do not work as well in the forex market and therefore need adapting. For example, I have increasingly noticed that in recent times the first attempt of a price breakout more often than not results in a failure.

The strategies that I am going to share with you are suitable for trading the forex market in any time frame – ranging from minutes to weeks. Throughout the book I also explain certain aspects of the forex market so that you can gain an insight into how the market behaves.

Even though each strategy has its own general guidelines, do note that all these strategies are open to individual customisation – flexibility is one of the key ingredients of becoming a successful trader. Flexibility is required for the trader to adapt his or her strategies to different market conditions, as well as for the trader to customise trading strategies to suit his or her own trading style and personality. Therefore, feel free to tweak or modify any of the parameters of these strategies to suit your own preferences.

In my years of trading the forex market, I have found that consistent success came from basing my trading philosophy on three M's:

- Mind

- Money

- Method

While this book focuses primarily on the Method portion, I wish to emphasise that for any strategy to be profitable, mind mastery and money management must also be incorporated as part of a holistic approach in enhancing one's overall trading performance – as performance is not assessed based on just a few trades, but on a series of trades made over a specific period of time.

The 7 strategies in this book must be applied with discipline and a huge dose of common sense. Their rules and guidelines are not set in stone. What I provide is a guide to implementing these strategies so that you can tilt the odds of success to your side.

How this book is structured

The book contains the following chapters.

Getting Started

Find out why the forex market is constantly growing, and why an increasing number of people are turning to trade this particular asset class in their quest to accumulate wealth. For those who are new to trading, take a look at the differences between investing and trading, and the various choices of trading time frames.

Spot Forex Market Structure

The forex market has long been the exclusive playground of the big players, namely banks, institutional investors and hedge funds. But the playground is no longer restricted to just them; individuals can also participate in this speculative game. However, independent forex traders can be disadvantaged in some ways due to how the spot forex market is structured. It is essential to know where you, the trader, stand in the overall big picture.

How To Overcome The Odds Of Trading Forex

How are you going to tackle the odds that are stacked against you from the start in the forex trading business? In this chapter, I will highlight the three Ms that have brought me success in this field: Mind, Money and Method. Many traders, especially the inexperienced ones, are too fixated on finding the perfect trade setup, the perfect trading system or the strategy that never fails, thus neglecting the other more important aspects that are crucial to good trading performance.

Strategy 1 – Market Sentiment

The forex market is heavily driven by market sentiment, and it is market sentiment that influences traders' decisions by triggering certain emotions and thoughts. Find out what defines the current market sentiment, and how you can incorporate market sentiment analysis into your trading.

Strategy 2 – Trend Riding

There is so much more to riding trends than simply closing your eyes and buying at any point during an uptrend or short-selling at any point during a downtrend. This chapter shows you how you can jump on a trend when the trend is the most robust, rather than when it is about to end. This way you can ride a trend with a higher chance of success.

Strategy 3 – Breakout Fading

Many false breakouts occur in forex price charts, and the occurrence of these *fakeouts* provides the perfect opportunity for fading breakouts, that is, trading against those breakouts. In this chapter, I explain why most breakouts fail, and how you can identify high-probability fading opportunities.

Strategy 4 – Breakout Trading

When currency prices break out of certain price levels, a large sustained move in the direction of the breakout may occur, giving rise to a situation whereby big profits could potentially be captured in the least amount of time. The main problem with trading breakouts is that many of these breakout attempts fail. In this chapter I walk you through several guidelines of how you can better identify potential breakout opportunities for this strategy.

Strategy 5 – Decreased Volatility Breakout

This strategy is conceptually similar to the strategy of breakout trading, because in both cases the trader will be hoping for a successful price breakout. This particular strategy, however, requires that the forex market registers a period of relative calm and low volatility before the strategy is to be implemented.

Strategy 6 – Carry Trade

This is a fundamental trading strategy that is highly favoured by institutional investors. In this chapter, I explain how a carry trade works, and highlight some points which you should keep in mind when adopting this strategy in the forex market.

Strategy 7 – News Straddling

The forex market is extremely sensitive to economic and geopolitical news from around the world, especially those which relate to the industrialised countries. The underlying reason why news is so important to forex trading is that each new piece of information can potentially change the trader's perceptions of the current and/or future situation relating to the outlook of certain currency pairs. Find out how you can trade news releases with a higher probability of success.

Risk disclosure

Trading forex involves substantial risk, and there is always the potential for loss. Your trading results may vary. No representation is made that any information in this book will guarantee profits or prevent losses from trading forex. You should be aware that no trading strategy can guarantee profits.

Further information

For more information about my trading strategies, the proprietary PowerFX Course and other forex market information, please visit the following website where I also host a daily forex blog – www.GraceCheng.com

Introduction

There are many different ways of trading forex, such as spot forex, futures, options or spread-betting. This book, however, shall focus on the trading of spot forex. The most significant difference between spot forex and futures is that spot forex contracts are traded over-the-counter at no central location, while forex futures are traded on an exchange. This gives rise to another unique aspect of spot forex – the 24-hour non-stop action; this is one major reason why I enjoy trading spot forex. With round-the-clock trading a person in any time-zone can trade spot forex at any time – whether during the day or night.

The best career decision I have made was to trade forex full-time. Forex trading has brought me both financial and emotional satisfaction, even though my initial learning journey was long and arduous.

When I started in forex, I could only find one book on forex trading. Forex was not as popular as stocks or options trading, so there were very few articles in magazines that focused on this field. I spent the first one and a half years learning how to trade forex and honing my skills on a demo account, before progressing to a real account, when I became consistently profitable. The breakthrough came when I incorporated fundamental and sentiment analysis into my predominantly technical-based analysis.

Even though I was able to dedicate myself to full-time trading, I found the initial learning curve to be extremely steep, as I had no mentor and had to learn all the ways of losing in the market before I learnt how to profit from it. I hope that through this book, aspiring and current traders are able to fast-track their learning, and greatly improve their trading performance.

The forex markets have the promise of fast action and huge profits, but the risks are also great. It is estimated that over 90% of forex traders end up losing their trading capital. The good news is that most of these losses can be prevented by taking the time to learn how to trade the forex markets and by implementing careful money management.

TRADING
FOREX

7 Winning Strategies for Trading Forex

1 :
Getting
Started

1: Getting Started

Forex (or FX) refers to the foreign exchange markets, where currencies are traded. It is the biggest and fastest growing financial market in the world, with an average daily turnover of almost $2 trillion – many times the total traded volume of the US stock exchanges.

The forex market consists of a worldwide wired network of buyers and sellers of currencies, with trading all done over-the-counter (OTC), which means that there is no central exchange and clearinghouse where orders are matched. If you are looking for 24-hour action, you can find it in this global trading system, where no physical barriers exist and activity moves seamlessly from one major financial centre to another.

A reason why there is a veil of mystery over forex is that the market was once the exclusive playground of banks, hedge funds, corporations and financial institutions, where money changed hands for commercial and speculative purposes. However, forex has now expanded and is easily accessible to all traders with the rapid emergence of online currency trading platforms. Many of these platforms are well-equipped with free charting software, real-time news-feeds and easy-to-use order placing systems.

The wide availability of sophisticated technology has spawned a whole new level of foreign exchange, where self-directed (so-called "retail") traders can easily buy and sell currencies through an internet connection with a click of the mouse, dealing with invisible counter-parties on the other side of the transaction. This group of people (also known as *speculative traders*) engage in trading forex for the sole purpose of making profits.

Welcome to the new world of online forex trading.

The rapid fluctuations of currency exchange rates are what attract speculators to the forex market as currencies are highly sensitive, and thus react very fast to changing economic conditions of countries or regions, changing interest rates and political happenings around the world. Sometimes central banks of countries attempt to intervene in the forex market if the policy-makers feel that their country's currency is too strong or too weak for their own good. All these factors lead to high volatility of currency prices, which can be taken advantage of by traders who speculate on the direction and magnitude of the current and future price move.

I would like to point out that while movements in certain currency pairs can be quite volatile in nature, most major currencies generally move less than 1% daily, which is much lower than that of active stocks, which can easily move between 5-10% per day. For a rough guide of currency pairs and their relative volatility, refer to Figure 1.1 under "Warming Up" in the later part of this chapter.

Forex has increasingly become an extremely attractive alternative asset group for speculators to trade, in addition to the usual staple of stocks and futures.

Anyone can trade forex, but not every one can be profitable. That's the rule of any game – *not every one can win*.

Unique Characteristics of the Forex Market

There are many opportunities for you to profit from the forex market. For example, if you have an opinion that the Euro is going to rise in value against the US dollar, you can "long" the EUR/USD, which means to buy the pair in the hope that the exchange rate will go higher. You would then make a profit if EUR/USD appreciates, as you would be able to sell at a higher price than you have bought it at before. But if you think that the Euro will weaken against the US dollar (i.e., EUR/USD will go down), you can initiate a trade by selling EUR/USD (known as going "short"), so that if EUR/USD later does go down in value, you would be able to make a profit by buying back at a lower price.

When you hear someone talking about the "forex market", the chances are that he or she is referring to the spot forex market. The spot forex market is where a trader buys or sells a currency at the current price on the date of the contract for delivery within two business days. Of course, for most speculators, there is no real delivery of actual cash, and the way this is done is through rolling over of positions [more of this will be explained under "Warming Up" later in this chapter].

This and many other peculiarities give the spot forex market its own unique characteristics which make it an interesting market to trade.

I explain below some of the main characteristics of the spot forex market.

A global 24-hour market

The forex market operates worldwide and non-stop for five and a half days a week. Every day it moves along with the sun: beginning in Sydney, to Tokyo and then Singapore, through the late Asian afternoon when London and other European centres open just as Asian markets are preparing to close. The European open initiates the heaviest trading volume of the day and by afternoon in Europe, New York opens, followed by Chicago, then Los Angeles. Just as sunset signals the closing of the US market, sunrise in Sydney starts a brand new trading cycle all over again.

By contrast, with the stock and futures markets, one would need access to electronic communication networks (ECN) for pre-market trading, or would have to wait till the markets open – and open sometimes with a gap if there has been news while the markets are closed. Since the Asian session is usually quiet for currencies like the Euro or Swiss Franc, I use this time to do market research, calculate and set up my trades for the afternoon when the European markets open. This gives me ample time to digest the news of the night before and the morning itself, which allows me to anticipate the movements of currency pairs later on in the day.

Unparalleled liquidity

The forex market is the planet's most liquid market. With more than $2 trillion changing hands every day, traders have no worries about liquidity when it comes to trading any of the big-economy currencies: USD, GBP, EUR, CHF, JPY, CAD, AUD and NZD. This is especially the case when they are paired up with the US dollar – at least 80 percent of foreign exchange transactions have a dollar leg.

The London market accounts for almost one-third of the global total daily forex turnover, and thus tends to be the most volatile session of the day, with the majority of forex transactions completed during the London hours due to the market's liquidity and efficiency.

The unparalleled liquidity of forex translates into very little or almost no slippage when you trade during normal market conditions (not during news); there is rarely any discrepancy between the displayed price and the execution price.

Ability to go long or short anytime

Since currencies are always traded in pairs, when you are bullish on one currency, you are bearish on the other – and vice versa.

For example, if you are bullish on GBP/USD, you go long of it by buying Pounds and selling US dollars; but if you are bearish, you can short it by selling Pounds and buying US dollars. You can short a currency pair anytime you want, without any restrictions. This is different from some stock markets whereby short-selling is only allowed on an uptick, so it can be quite tedious and time-consuming for stock traders to have to wait and see the stocks going down while looking out for an uptick before they can short.

Being able to go long or short on currency pairs anytime is a tremendous advantage as forex traders are able to profit from both up and down trends anytime, and this translates to a more efficient and instant order execution. This is especially valuable in the financial markets where time equals money, and even a second's delay could cost you money.

Choice of high leverage

Who doesn't like trading on other people's money? With possible leverage of up to 400 times, the forex market indisputably offers the highest amount of leverage compared to other markets. This high end of leverage is usually offered to mini trading accounts, due to the smaller lot sizes and lower minimum account deposit requirements. With a 100 times margin-based leverage, that is typically offered for standard-sized accounts, forex traders are allowed to execute trades of up to $100,000 with an initial margin of only $1000.

It is important to note that while a high degree of leverage allows traders to maximise their profit potential, especially on a small price move, the potential for loss is equally large. Many people mistakenly shy away from trading forex after hearing that it is a highly leveraged trading instrument, but these people do not realise that leverage is and can be customised to the individual trader's own preference. If you tend to be more conservative with risk-taking, you may choose to use no more than 10 times leverage, or none at all. For those of you with more aggressive risk appetite, you can choose a higher amount of leverage in your trades. The choice of leverage lies with you.

Lower costs

Since forex transactions are done the OTC way, with traders dealing directly with the market maker or other parties, exchange and clearing fees are not applicable to forex trading. Market makers typically do not charge commissions on trades that are executed through them, while Electronic Network Communications (ECN) do charge a small commission on top of the bid-and-ask spread.

Due to the high level of liquidity in the market, currency pairs usually have very tight spreads especially during normal market conditions when no news is scheduled for release.

Investing vs Trading

There are some important differences between investing and trading, even though some people may use these terms interchangeably without giving it much thought of what each entails. Advantages can be found in both ways of growing your money, neither is better than the other – they have different roles.

But when it comes to growing your wealth in the forex market, trading is usually the way to go due to the unique aspects of this market.

Value ownership

Investors are concerned with acquiring the ownership of the financial instrument; they have the confidence that the instrument will continue to rise in value. They tend to "buy low and sell high". For example, when they see that the stock price is going down, they may see it as a good opportunity to buy and own the stock 'cheaply' so that they may profit when the stock goes back higher in the future.

Traders, on the other hand, do not have much concern with the buying and owning of the instrument. They exhibit the same ease with either longing (buying) or short-selling the instrument. Unlike investors, traders are more willing to buy 'high' in the hope of being able to sell even 'higher', or short-sell 'low' in the hope of being able to buy back later at an even 'lower' price.

Time frame

Investing usually entails the "buy and hold" concept, whereby an investor's goal is to acquire a financial instrument and to hold it for medium to long term, in the hope that the instrument will rise in significant value after a certain period of time. Trading couldn't be any more different. In trading, a trader's main goal is to profit whichever way the market goes, whether upward or downward, within a shorter time frame. While there is short and long term trading, the holding period rarely extends beyond more than a few months, or longer than a year.

Getting in

Serious investors tend to buy an instrument based on the underlying fundamental reasons. For instance, savvy stock investors will analyze the background of a company, pour over its quarterly earnings report, assess the company's reputation and strength in the particular industry sector, and assess the potential of its products and the track record of the management team. Traders, however, tend to look for high-probability trade setups using technical analysis as their favourite tool, and many of them also incorporate market sentiment into their trading decisions. Short-term traders are quick to recognise changing market trends, and take advantage of price swings in the market, whether in range-bound or trending environments.

Getting out

The "buy and hold" mentality of investors tends not to deviate far from "buy and forget", as many investors almost have zilch idea of when to get out of their investment when things do not go well. Many stock investors are left with worthless stocks as they do not have stop-loss boundaries or know when to cut their losses. While there are also many traders out there who do not have risk management rules in place, traders overall are generally more aware of proper risk management than most investors. Whether or not they translate these rules into practice is another thing altogether.

Trading Time Frames

Before you enter into a position, you need to know – beforehand – when you are going to exit the market. A trader is not going to hold onto a position indefinitely, that's for sure. Knowing the time frame of how long you wish to hold onto your open position will determine your exit points and prices. If you choose to hold a position for, say, a week, your profit objective would naturally be higher than if you were to hold it for a few hours because you would expect the price to move further, given the longer period of time.

This is a personal decision which has to be made by the trader, depending on his or her risk tolerance level, lifestyle desired, and the amount of time to be dedicated to analyzing the market.

There are mainly four different types of trading time frames:

1. scalping

2. day trading

3. swing trading

4. position trading

These are explained below.

1. Scalping

This is the shortest time frame in trading; it exploits small changes in currency prices. It describes the ultra-rapid action of opening and closing of a position within a few seconds or minutes, with the aim of stealing a few pips from each trade. The profit of the winning trade is small, while the number of such winning trades should be big enough so that these small profits can add up to a decent amount.

Scalpers usually need to have access to the tightest spreads and fastest connection speeds possible, in order to carry out this bullet-speed trading with the tiny profits. They tend to do this many times a day so as to accumulate the little profits that are harvested.

Losses must be limited such that one large loss does not wipe out the profits gained from many winning trades.

Many forex market makers discourage this type of trading as they find it difficult to cover the opposite side of the transactions, given the fast speed and numerous orders entered into their systems.

2. Day trading

Day trading is one of the more popular types of trading, whereby traders open and close positions within a day. They also do not hold their positions overnight because of the added risk of not knowing if prices would change dramatically while they sleep. The holding period of their trades may range from minutes to hours.

Day trading relies heavily on intraday momentum to bring the current price to the desired price level in one direction. Day traders are looking out for signs that a currency pair has a high probability of moving in a particular direction, going from point X to point Y, within a day regardless of whether the price is moving in a trend or range.

Day traders tend to wait for good trading opportunities, instead of trading frantically like scalpers tend to do. This style of trading involves intense concentration from the trader as positions must be closely monitored on the price charts.

3. Swing trading

Swing traders hold their positions for a few days, but seldom more than a week. Identifying and riding on trends early is the central objective of this trading style, and the profit objective tends to be set higher than that of day trading since the swing trader is expecting that by holding out for a few days, there is a better chance of capturing a larger price move. Unlike the day trader, the swing trader has to endure overnight risk.

As swing trading requires much less minute-to-minute monitoring of the market, this type of trading is generally preferred by people who hold day jobs.

My opinion is that swing traders must still keep up-to-date with the latest fundamental and technical changes in the market, even when they are not monitoring the market all the time.

4. Position trading

Position trading spans the longest period of time, and refers to traders holding their position for weeks or even months. Position traders seek to identify and trade currency pairs that signal that a medium to long term trend is playing out – but will take more than a few days to play out. Their positions are usually closed before the trend runs out of power. This trading time frame is the least time-consuming one among all the different ones, as there is not much need for intensive monitoring. Many position traders place a trailing stop which automatically closes their position if the price retraces past a particular point.

Choosing a time-frame

As a general rule of thumb: the smaller the time frame you trade then the more time is needed to be devoted to monitoring the markets.

Someone who day trades tends to be more in touch with the price swings and goings-on of the market as positions are opened and closed during the same day. Whereas at the end of the spectrum, a position trader does not have to monitor the market so intensively.

Risk-wise, I would say that the longer the time frame used in trading, the more risk has to be assumed by the trader. This is simply because the market has more time to move against them, and can move much further against them than it can in a smaller time frame.

Many of the strategies mentioned in this book are meant for short-term trading. However, you may decide on the length of your holding period to suit your personal preference by adjusting the profit target and stop-loss accordingly. Of course, the size of profit objective and stop-loss will be proportional to the length of your holding period – the shorter your time frame, the smaller your profit target and stop-loss should be; the longer the trading time frame, the wider your profit target and stop-loss can be.

Warming Up

Opening an account

How do I set up an account?

Before you set up a trading account to trade forex, you first need to choose which forex broker best suits your needs and trading style. There are mainly two types of brokers:

1. ECN (Electronic Communication Network) and

2. Market-Maker

[These will be explained further in Chapter 2.]

It is very important to make sure that the broker is situated in a country where their activities can be monitored by a regulatory agency.

Experiment first with virtual money

The best way to learn how to trade forex and to see if it is suitable for you is to trade it real-time, but with a demo account initially. Demo accounts can be opened for free with certain brokers; no real money is deposited in this type of account. You can experiment real-time trading with different currency pairs using various trading strategies without losing any real money – it is a good way to build up some confidence. You can get a sense of how it feels to have a profit or a loss, even though the intensity of these emotions will be of a different level when trading with real money. It is the best way for new traders to dip their toes in the water.

How much money is needed to start?

The amount of trading capital needed is relative. After getting a feel with a demo account, you can start with real money. The first type of account you can open is a mini account which requires a minimum of just a few hundred US dollars (some brokers even allow you to open a mini account with just US$100). However, don't expect to grow rich on such a small amount. For standard-sized accounts, the general minimum is around a few thousand US dollars.

Thinking of putting your life savings into a trading account?

Don't. Only trade with money you can afford to lose. Make sure that even if you lose all of your trading capital, your lifestyle won't be affected.

If you lose a large amount, you may never want to trade again. Whereas if you lose virtual money in a demo account, or a small amount in a mini account, it may be easier to pick yourself back up after losses – both emotionally and financially.

Currency codes

Each currency is represented by a three-letter currency code according to the International Organisation for Standardisation (ISO). The ISO 4217 code list defines different currencies, and is the standard used in the banking industry and in businesses all around the world. See below for some of the more common currency codes.

The first two letters of the currency code are based on the two letters of the country code according to the ISO 3166-1 alpha-2 (they are also often used to denote a country's domain on the Internet) and the third letter is usually the initial of the currency itself. For example, Canada's currency code is CAD – CA for Canada and D for dollar.

Table 1.1: Common ISO currency codes	
Some Common ISO Currency Codes	
US Dollar	USD
British Pound	GBP
Euro	EUR
Japanese Yen	JPY
Swiss Franc	CHF
Canadian Dollar	CAD
Australian Dollar	AUD
New Zealand Dollar	NZD
[A more comprehensive list of currency codes can be found in the appendix.]	

Currencies are traded in pairs

When a currency is bought, another currency must be sold in exchange, and, conversely, when a currency is sold, another currency must be bought in exchange. This act of simultaneous buying and selling is the most important aspect of forex: a currency is always traded against another currency. Thus currencies are always traded in pairs – for example, the US dollar and the Japanese Yen (USD/JPY) or the Euro and the US dollar (EUR/USD). The first currency in the pair is known as the base currency, and the second currency is the counter or terms currency.

Trade size

In some forex trading platforms, trades are executed in standard sizes of 10,000 base currency per one lot, but in other platforms, trades are executed in standard sizes of 100,000 base currency per one lot. Therefore, there is no universal definition of what a "standard-sized" lot is, even though a "standard lot" typically refers to a trade size of 100,000 base currency units in the realm of retail currency trading. There is usually no maximum trading size, but some brokers require that you request for a quote over the telephone for trading sizes bigger than 10,000,000 base currency units.

Pips

What are pips?

"Pips" will be one of the most common words that you will use when you trade forex. The term *pip* stands for *percentage in point*. It represents the smallest incremental move an exchange rate can make. For example, 1 pip is 0.0001 for USD/CHF, or 0.01 for USD/JPY.

How to calculate pip values

In currency pairs where the counter currency (the second symbol in a pair) is the US dollar, for example, EUR/USD, GBP/USD or AUD/USD, one pip always equals US$10, for every 100,000 currency units. For other currency pairs, where the USD is the base currency (the first symbol in a pair), one pip will usually be worth less than US$10 for every 100,000 currency units, and it varies slightly due to fluctuating exchange rates.

Here is the formula that is used to calculate pip value:

```
Value of a pip = (one pip, with the appropriate decimal
placement/currency exchange rate) x (trade amount)
```

Note that the two variables are the exchange rate and the trade amount.

Variable Pip Value

Let's say you want to calculate how much one pip is worth for US$100,000 of USD/CHF at the time when the USD/CHF exchange rate is around 1.2200.

```
Pip value = (0.0001/1.2200) x US$100,000
          = US$8.19
```

Therefore, if you have made 30 pips on US$100,000 worth of USD/CHF trade, your profit would be 30 x US$8.19 = US$245.70.

Here is another example.

Let's say you want to calculate how much one pip is worth for US$100,000 of USD/JPY at the time when the USD/JPY exchange rate is around 119.20.

```
Pip value = (0.01/119.20) x US$100,000
          = US$8.38
```

Notice that:

- one pip in USD/JPY is expressed as 0.01 because the exchange rate of USD/JPY has two decimal places, but

- one pip in USD/CHF is expressed as **0.0001** because the exchange rate of USD/CHF has *four decimal places*.

Fixed Pip Value

Now, let us calculate how much one pip is worth for 100,000 Euros of EUR/USD at the time when the EUR/USD exchange rate is around 1.3000.

```
Pip value = (0.0001/1.3000) x EUR100,000
          = EUR7.69
```

As you have noticed, the value is in Euros. So to convert the pip value from Euros to US dollars, you multiply EUR7.69 by the current EUR/USD exchange rate, which is 1.3000 in this example.

```
Pip value = EUR7.69 x 1.3000
          = US$10.00
```

This two-step calculation explains why the pip value is *always* US$10 per 100,000 currency units for currency pairs that quote the USD as the counter currency.

So if you have traded £100,000 worth of GBP/USD, and you have a 20 pip profit, you would get 20 x US$10, which is US$200 profit.

Reading forex rates

A market maker will usually quote a *two-way* market price – "two-way" meaning a bid and an ask price–

- a *bid* is a price at which a market maker is willing to **buy** a currency (and at which the trader is willing to sell), while

- an *ask* is a price at which a market maker is willing to **sell** a currency (and at which the trader is willing to buy).

Here are some examples of currency quotes:

EUR/USD 1.3000 / 1.3003
USD/CHF 1.2236 / 1.2240
GBP/USD 1.9500 / 1.9504

The quote on the left-hand side is the bid, whereas the one on the right-hand side is the ask. As you can see, the ask is always higher than the bid, and the difference (which is called the *spread*) is where the market maker makes its money from. In the example of the EUR/USD quote above, the spread is 3 pips.

Based on the GBP/USD quote above, you can sell £1 for US$1.9500 according to the bid price, or you can buy £1 for US$1.9504 according to the ask price.

Understanding rollover

Forex transactions in the spot market are always due for settlement two business days later. So if a trader sells a certain quantity of a currency on, say, Monday, he or she is obligated to deliver that quantity of the currency on Wednesday. However, in practice, when you buy and sell currencies in the spot market as a retail trader you don't really take delivery of the actual currency. This is because you are likely to be trading on a leveraged trading account, which means you can get a loan from your forex broker for the amount that you are trading.

For example, if you want to buy or sell $100,000 worth of a currency, you may only need to pay $1000 for the deal if your broker allows a 1% margin. So to avoid taking actual delivery of the currency that you have bought or sold, most forex brokers will automatically roll over your positions to the next business day by closing your position and opening an identical one with a delivery date within the next two days.

Rollover is usually done on a daily basis at 5:00 pm New York time, and only affects those who hold their positions overnight.

During rollover, the broker pays or charges you whatever the interest rate differential is between the two currencies in the pair. So if you have bought (long) a particular currency, and that currency has a higher overnight interest rate than the counter currency, you will gain the difference. If you have sold (short) the currency with a higher overnight interest rate, then you will be charged the difference. The broker also keeps a percentage of this rollover for itself, which is why the amount you receive will always be less than what you must pay for a given currency pair.

Most brokers also have a slightly strange way of dealing with the weekend rollover. Rather than charging you the 2 non-trading days of Saturday and Sunday on the night of Friday, they usually charge it on a Wednesday. This can be somewhat confusing for new traders who wonder why their rollover is so much higher on a Wednesday than on other days of the week.

Some brokers may also call the rollover payout or charge the "swap", as a swap is the term used for an interest rate differential between two currencies over a given period of time.

What sort of leverage can I get?

Leverage involves borrowing a certain amount of the money needed to invest in something. In the case of forex, that money is usually borrowed from a broker. Forex trading does offer high leverage in the sense that for an initial margin requirement, you can build up and control a huge trading position.

Margin is the minimum required balance to place a trade. Forex brokers set their own margin requirements, which typically range from 1-2% of the value of the position.

For example, if you want to trade $100,000 of USD/CHF and the margin required is 1%, or $1000, your margin-based leverage will be 100 times, which is derived by dividing the total transaction value by the margin required.

Many retail forex brokers offer a sizeable amount of leverage to their customers. Some offer 50 times leverage, while an increasing number of them even allow up to 400 times leverage for standard-sized or mini-sized accounts. It is very important to know that leverage magnifies both your profits and losses. The good thing is that you, the customer, are often given the flexibility to select your leverage amount.

Trading

Slippage

Slippage occurs when your order gets executed at a price different from what you were expecting (or hoping). This can easily occur in fast-moving markets, usually during or after some news release, for any non-limit orders.

Liquidity

Even though forex has the greatest liquidity in the financial markets, it does not mean that all currency pairs have the same liquidity. The table below shows the relative liquidity of some important currency pairs.

Table 1.2: liquidity of major currency pairs	
Currency Pair	Liquidity
EUR/USD	High
EUR/JPY	High
USD/JPY	High
USD/CHF	Medium
GBP/USD	Medium
USD/CAD	Medium
NZD/USD	Low
AUD/USD	Low

Volatility

Some currency pairs are more volatile than others. While some pairs can easily move at least 130 pips in a day, other pairs only manage to move less than 70 pips a day.

The figure over the page shows the average daily volatility in some important currency pairs. In this case *volatility* is measured in terms of pips moved in a day. This is not the conventional way of measuring volatility, which is usually done by measuring the percentage move of a pair in a given time frame. However, since most traders look at the pip move, I am showing volatility in terms of what is most easily measured by traders.

The more a currency pair moves in a day, the greater the chance that profits can be made within a day. Currency pairs which tend to move more than 100 pips a day (for example, GBP/USD and USD/CHF) usually catch the fancy of day traders because they offer the best opportunities for capturing decent-sized profits in a shorter period of time.

The broad spectrum of volatility ensures that there is something to suit everyone, ranging from the aggressive to the conservative trader. The currency pair that you choose to concentrate your trading on will depend on how aggressive or conservative you are.

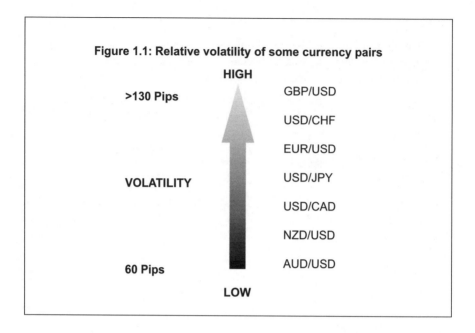

Figure 1.1: Relative volatility of some currency pairs

HIGH

>130 Pips   GBP/USD

USD/CHF

EUR/USD

VOLATILITY   USD/JPY

USD/CAD

NZD/USD

60 Pips   AUD/USD

LOW

Common types of order

There is a great range of orders that traders can give to precisely control the execution of their order. Not all brokers will accept the same range of order types, but I list below the most common types of orders that most brokers should accept.

Market Order

An order to buy or sell at the current market price.

Limit Order

An order to buy or sell at a specified price or better.

Stop-Loss Order

An order to close a position if the market price hits a certain level. Note however, that this type of order means that after the stop price is hit the order becomes a market order and you may suffer slippage.

Limit Entry Order

An order to buy below the market or sell above the market at a specified price. You use this type of entry order if you feel that the currency pair will reverse direction from that price.

Stop-Entry Order

An order to buy above the market or sell below the market at a specified price. You use this type of entry order if you feel that the currency pair will continue in the same direction. Just like with a stop order, you may suffer slippage when using this type of order.

Stop-Limit Order

An order to buy above the market or sell below the market at a specified price only. When your price is hit your order becomes a limit order which prevents slippage. However, there is a chance that in a fast-moving market your order won't be filled at all.

One Triggers Other (OTO)/ Parent and Contingent

A set of orders whereby when the parent order is filled, the contingent order is placed. This is commonly used to make sure a stop and/or limit order is placed as soon as an entry order is filled.

One Cancels Other (OCO)

A set of orders whereby when one order is filled, the other order is cancelled. This is commonly used to set both a profit-taking limit order and a stop-loss order as soon as an entry order is filled.

How to Choose a Broker

The forex broker that you use can significantly affect your trading success.

There are two types of forex brokers: market makers and ECNs. But in practice things are not so clear-cut – there are market makers out there who falsely market themselves as not having dealing desks, while there are also some brokers who claim to be true ECNs when they are not.

The choice of broker must be an individual decision, because everyone has different needs and preferences. Both new and existing traders should carefully examine the practices and policy contracts of brokers, and be up-to-date with new information on brokers.

Below are some points that you might want to consider when selecting a broker. You can use it as a rough guide to narrow down some candidates that match your own needs.

Broker type

- Do you prefer to trade with a market maker or an ECN?

Security

- How safe are your funds with them?

Broker location

- Is the broker regulated by any regulatory authority in that country? [Refer to the appendix for a list of main regulatory organisations.] Note that even if the broker is regulated, no entity can completely guarantee the safety of client funds.

- Are the client funds insured against fraud, theft, or embezzlement?

- Are the funds maintained separately from the broker's operating funds? Even if the broker says that the funds are kept separate, it does not mean that they are segregated as defined according to certain agencies' regulations.

Trial account

- Does the broker provide a trial demo account?

Trading platform

- How many different currency pairs can you trade?

- Does it come with any charting interface? Can you trade from the charts?

- Are you comfortable with the order placing system?

- Do they have one-click trading? This will be useful when scalping.

- Is order execution instant and efficient? This will be especially crucial if you are scalping.

- Does it freeze during times of news releases or when the market is moving very fast?

- If you want to implement your own automated trading system, does it offer an Application Programming Interface (API)?

- Will you need to trade while on the move? If so, check if it has a mobile or web-based version that you can use for trading.

Account and trade size

- What is the minimum amount that is required for opening an account?

- What is the minimum trade size? 10,000 or 100,000 currency units?

- Can you make adjustments to the lot size traded?

- What is the maximum size you can trade without having to call for a quote?

- What is the maximum size they will guarantee your orders be filled at? Or, if it is an ECN, how easy is it to fill big orders?

Order types and handling

- What order types are supported? Do they support Stop, Limit, Stop-Limit, One-Triggers-Other (OTO) and One-Cancels-Other (OCO) orders?

- How much slippage do you get when trading during news releases?

- Find out the broker's policy on stop-loss and limit orders. Depending on the policy, it is possible to end up with closing prices that are worse than expected.

Commissions and spreads

- ECNs generally charge a commission when you open and close your positions. Are you willing to accept that?

- Are spreads fixed or variable?

If spreads are variable, how wide do they get during important news releases?

Margin

- What is the margin percentage? The lower the margin required, the greater the amount of leverage.

- Is the margin requirement identical for mini and standard accounts?

Once you have narrowed the broker list down to a few candidates, be sure to read the terms and conditions of the respective contracts, and understand what you are in for before you sign anything. Later on when you have graduated to an intermediate or advanced phase in trading forex, you may then choose to spread your money among a few brokers so as to reduce exposure to a single broker.

Forex Trading Is A Serious Business

Forex trading must be seen as a serious business, not just a casual roll of the dice or a leisurely pursuit. If you approach trading as a means of getting your dose of adrenaline, do yourself a favour by staying away from it – you will do less harm to your pockets by going to the latest Louis Vuitton sale or by bidding on that vintage car on eBay for the adrenaline shot.

Serious money demands serious work. Winners from the trading arena take a no-nonsense approach to trading – they take care of their P&L (profits and losses), enter only into high probability trades and keep meticulous record of all their trades.

Both serious and casual traders, of course, dream of making it big in the forex market, but it is not the goal that counts, it is the preparation and dedication that is important. Forex trading should be considered and treated as a serious business, just like other types of businesses. Approaching trading from the perspective of a shrewd business person can greatly tilt your chances of success to your side.

A Day in the Life of a Full-Time Forex Trader

Middle of the night

An alarm from my computer rings. Jolted from sleep, I drag my feet – with eyes half-open – into my trading room. I turn on the LCD monitors and look immediately at the screen showing the 5-minute chart of GBP/USD. The time is 2:10am and the FOMC minutes have just been released. GBP/USD has fallen by around 40 pips so far to 1.9730 – an intraday low.

I click on the headline which summarises what the minutes say. It seems that the Fed's main concern is that inflation will fail to moderate as expected, and that future policy adjustments will depend on incoming economic data. This statement is very similar to the previous one; hence there is not much reaction in the forex market. Both EUR/USD and USD/CHF barely move more than 20 pips. I wait a few more minutes to see how the price action in GBP/USD will unfold, but when I see that the currency pair is losing momentum, I switch off the monitors and go back to bed. The price is not where I want to buy GBP/USD.

Morning

Too soon, morning comes. I start off the day by having breakfast in front of one of my computers, looking at screens that show the 5-minute charts USD/CHF, EUR/USD, USD/JPY and GBP/USD. These four currency pairs (also known as "majors") are what I usually check out the first thing in the morning, unless I've got a position open in other currency pairs. I quickly scroll through the news headlines that are displayed in the news feeds, and select those which relate directly to forex. Sometimes there are tons of press reports to read, other times there isn't much, and today there is a sprinkle of reports written by financial news journalists who are all trying to dissect what the Fed is up to.

The analysis that I had done yesterday threw up some significant support and resistance levels in USD/CHF, and since I'm not expecting any big price breakouts in the meantime, I place some limit orders near them. As much as I am eager for some fast-moving actions in the market, most currency pairs still haven't moved much during the time I was asleep, since the release of FOMC minutes several hours ago. The market seems pretty boring at this time.

The lull in market activity gives me some time to write a bit more of this book, and to work on some trading articles.

Lunch

Later on, just as I am getting ready to go out for lunch with a friend, I see that USD/CHF is moving up toward a specific resistance level, and my short position (to sell-short instead of buying) could be open very soon. To make sure the trade is still sound, I quickly check the news feeds to see if any news or rumours might have triggered this move.

As it moves closer to my price point, I decide to leave the short order in place as the move doesn't seem to be triggered by any news. The market is moving up and closer to my position; it is now only one pip away. I make sure all my charts are up, and I prepare to monitor this trade. Suddenly, USD/CHF seems to move down. I wonder if I've missed the opportunity. It is now 12 pips away from my opening price, a bit too late for me to get in.

And just as suddenly as the price has gone down, it is now moving up again and my order is now filled. It seems I haven't missed out on the move after all. Now my only fear is that USD/CHF could break out successfully from that resistance point. The pair keeps moving up, 5 pips then 10. I am now in loss, but I'm not too worried since the actual resistance point hasn't been reached yet as it is still 5 pips away.

Non-lunch

The up move on USD/CHF seems to be slowing down a bit. I guess others must be going short too. After what seems like an eternity, but is probably no more than five minutes, my position is back at break-even, which means I have neither made nor lost money at this point. This bounce trade seems to be taking a while, so I call my friend to let her know we will have to postpone our lunch meeting. Lunch will have to arrive in the form of junk food from my favorite food delivery outlet. Sometimes I watch my open trade like a hawk; other times, I simply continue with other activities.

I set some price alarms and get back to writing my book while waiting for my lunch. After all, it is usually better to do something else while waiting on the market. That way, a trader won't feel as bored and it prevents him or her from trading out of boredom.

After lunch, the alarms ring. I look at the charts and see that USD/CHF is moving down sharply. Looks like I am close to reaching my profit target. Institutional traders must be back from lunch and are taking profits on their long positions. Finally, to my delight, within the next half hour, my short USD/CHF trade reaches the profit objective.

End of the day

With this trade out of the way, I look for upcoming trading opportunities. They are all quite far from the current price, so I embark on the regular routine of blogging on my website about the latest developments in the market and their implications, and capture some chart screenshots to include in the post. Trading blogs, especially those that have fresh and relevant material, can be a valuable source of useful and targeted information for busy traders who hold day jobs. This blogging habit, which constitutes part of my market homework, has helped me in my own trading. I also take the time to interact with the online community of traders by participating in forums such as that as ForexVibes (www.forexvibes.com).

Trading is unlike a 9-to-5 job; there isn't a fixed time for the start or the end of my daily trading activities. This means that sometimes I will end past midnight, and other times I will be done well before lunch time.

2:
Spot Forex
Market Structure

2: Spot Forex Market Structure

The spot forex market has always been a decentralised global network of buyers and sellers – meaning there is no physical central exchange that acts as a central clearing party. This is unlike, say, stocks or futures which traded through the exchanges such the London Stock Exchange or Chicago Mercantile Exchange.

Trading of currencies is done OTC (over-the-counter), in the sense that currency buyers and sellers from all over the world make a binding contract with each other after agreeing on a price – and this is not carried out through an exchange. This aspect of spot forex trading is different from forex futures trading which *is* carried out through an exchange. Forex traders carry out their activities by dealing directly with one another or through brokers via telephone and internet connections.

FXMarketSpace

In early 2007, the Chicago Mercantile Exchange (CME) and Reuters launched the world's first centrally cleared global forex market place called FXMarketSpace.

There are several benefits of a central exchange, for example:

- **counterparty risk** for trades is reduced, and

- there is **trading anonymity** – something very much coveted, especially for big players.

In this centrally cleared system, the CME will act as the central counterparty and guarantee the performance of all contracts for both buyers and sellers. Unfortunately, FXMarketSpace is an institutional trading platform and is not open to retail market players. According to the website (www.fxmarketspace.com), market participants would have to meet the FSA (Financial Services Authority is based in the United Kingdom) definition of a "Market Counterparty", and individuals would have to be sophisticated investors, typically with a net worth over $20 million. Therefore, as a central exchange for forex retail players is still not a reality, I shall focus on the OTC structure of the forex market in this chapter.

Market Players

The OTC nature of the forex market means that currency transactions do not converge at one single place, but instead are conducted all over the globe. Players of the forex market range from those who trade billions of dollars a day, to those who trade just tens of thousands of dollars.

A player's access to the forex market depends on their quantity of transactions of large amounts of money. The world's big banks are the main market players, and they form the exclusive club where most trading activities take place. This club is known as the *interbank market*. The more money you have, or are able to get a credit for, the more likely you are able to access this big boys' club.

Down the hierarchy are the smaller banks, big multinational companies, hedge funds and other institutional investors or speculators, and retail forex brokers. These large speculators may also conduct currency transactions directly in the interbank market, if they deal in large amounts and have credit standings with the large banks.

Next in line are the independent retail traders who lie at the bottom of the market structure. These individual traders mainly trade through forex brokers as they generally trade in much smaller lot sizes.

Central banks of countries are also market players, although they are not always involved in the market.

See Figure 2.1 for a basic illustration of the forex market structure.

Figure 2.1: forex market structure

A basic illustration of the forex market structure. Hedge funds and companies are not included in this illustration as the retail trader will usually not deal directly with any of them.

Banks

Who makes the currency prices in the market?

Without a central exchange, currency exchange rates are made, or set, by market makers – they make the bid and the ask prices based on the currency movements that they anticipate will take place. The largest banks are the major market makers, and they handle very large forex transactions – often in the billions of dollars – on behalf of their clients, such as other institutions or companies, and also for themselves. Many banks have traders dedicated to trading speculatively for the bank.

The resulting massive flows of money handled by these large banks are what primarily drive currency prices. This big money-laden network forms the interbank market where large banks deal with one another, and is where most of the trading activity takes place.

The transactions carried out by these major banks amount to the greatest bulk of the total daily forex volume. These big banks include Citigroup, Barclays Capital, UBS and Deutsche Bank.

Brokering platforms

The banks deal with one another directly, or through electronic brokering platforms like the Electronic Brokering Services (EBS) or Reuters Dealing 3000 Matching. These brokering systems get the best available exchange rates for the various currency pairs, and match buying and selling requests from bank dealers. Between these two competitors, they connect at least 1000 banks together.

In order to deal with each other, banks must have specific credit lines with each other since there is no exchange to serve as each bank's counterparty.

As main market makers, they constantly quote a bid and an ask price to one another, thereby "making" the market. Smaller banks that trade smaller amounts also get access to these brokering platforms.

Large companies

Companies and businesses are involved in the forex market because of their need to pay for products and services which are denominated in other currencies. Since these commercial entities deal in smaller quantities, compared to that of large banks, they usually trade through banks instead of directly accessing the interbank market themselves.

Large overall trade flows can have a significant impact on the forex market, as they play a role in the supply and demand of currencies.

Besides paying for goods and services in the normal course of doing business, many large multinational companies are also players in the forex market due to their hedging activities.

Sometimes companies may also be involved in currency speculation for the purpose of generating additional revenue.

Cross-border mergers and acquisitions (M&A) of companies can also have an impact, albeit a very short-term one, on currency prices. M&As tend to involve a huge amount of money, often in the billions. Currency conversions must take place if the M&A deal relates to companies from different countries, and involves cash transactions. Major cross-border M&A deals can influence the trading decisions of institutional speculators as they anticipate a temporary shift in supply and demand of the currencies involved.

Central banks

Central banks hold the key to controlling the supply and demand of national currencies; hence they play a very important role in the forex markets.

Examples of some prominent central banks include the US Federal Reserve Bank (the Fed), the European Central Bank (ECB), the Bank of England (BOE) and the Bank of Japan (BOJ) – with the Fed undoubtedly being the most influential among all the other central banks in the world.

Issues that are of most concern to central banks are those relating to: inflation (price stability), economic growth and the unemployment rate. One of the ways that central banks control these factors is through the setting and adjustment of interest rates, which will affect the valuation of many currencies.

Sometimes central banks intervene directly in the forex market when they are not satisfied with the current exchange rates of their currencies. That is, they may find that the current exchange rate is either too high or too low for the overall benefit of the economy.

The Bank of Japan is well-known for its intervention in the market. As Japan's economic backbone lies in its exporting activities, a weaker Yen is more beneficial in stimulating exports. Hence, when the BOJ deems that the Yen is getting much stronger against, say, the US dollar or the Euro, it may step into the open market to deliberately depress its currency by selling Yen against US dollars and Euros. This act of central bank intervention may cause other institutional players to follow suit, and further drive the currency exchange rate towards the rate that is favoured by the intervening central bank.

Besides direct intervention, policymakers from central banks may also occasionally use verbal comments about the desired state of their currency exchange rate when they are worried about the currency's excessive strength and volatility so that the exchange rate may be in line with the monetary policy of the central bank.

Institutional investors/speculators

Institutional investors/speculators include hedge funds and investment management companies. Most of these institutional speculators have international portfolios that consist of both domestic and international assets like stock or bonds to diversify their holdings. They tend to be very aggressive participants of the spot forex market as they often facilitate currency transactions when purchasing or selling foreign assets. For example, an investment manager who is in charge of an international stock portfolio will be required to buy and sell foreign currencies so as to pay for any purchase of overseas stocks.

Hedge funds, being largely unregulated, often practise very different styles of wealth generation from investment management companies; they tend to adopt more aggressive forms of trading with the aim of generating a high return on investment. Sometimes, a portion of their assets under management may be allocated specifically for currency speculations, with the objective of maximising their overall profits.

Large hedge funds and investment management companies are capable of moving the forex market in their transactions. The most unforgettable example of a hedge fund leaving its legacy in history is when George Soros's Quantum Fund made an estimated $1 billion in profit by betting that the British Pound would be forced out of the European Exchange Rate Mechanism. Subsequently, Soros became known as "the man who broke the Bank of England".

Forex brokers

The emergence of sophisticated online forex brokers made forex trading feasible for private individuals. In the past, only wealthy individuals could speculate in the forex market, but now things are very different. Anyone can simply open a trading account with a retail forex broker and trade currencies online with little money upfront, as forex brokers tend to offer highly leveraged margin accounts for individuals. There are basically two types of forex brokers:

1. market makers: who set the bid and the ask prices themselves, and

2. Electronic Communication Networks (ECNs): consolidate various bid and ask prices from market makers and other participants connected to their platform, and display the best available prices.

These are explained in some detail below.

1. Market Makers

Market-making is a lucrative business for banks and brokers, and forms the backbone of market liquidity. By quoting the bid and the ask prices on the screens of electronic brokering platforms, or through telephone calls, they are essentially providing liquidity and inviting other qualified parties (other banks, hedge funds, corporations or retail customers like individual traders) to deal with them. In doing so, market makers must be prepared to buy or sell from other market participants.

For example, if someone wants to buy a specified amount of EUR/USD from them at the agreed rate, the market maker must sell the requested amount to them at the ask price, thus making them the counterparty to the transaction.

Some market makers may have established credit links with banks that trade on the interbank market, or they access electronic brokering platforms like EBS or Reuters for pricing.

Bid/ask spread

Through market-making, market makers profit from the bid/ask spread, which is the difference between:

1.   the price at which the market maker will buy (bid price), and the

2.   price at which it will sell at (ask price) from a customer.

For example, if the bid price for EUR/USD is 1.2700 and the ask price is 1.2702, then the spread based on these prices will be 0.0002 or 2 pips.

During periods of high liquidity in which there is a great deal of trading activity, spreads of the actively traded currency pairs are usually kept quite narrow, between 1-4 pips. When the market is very quiet with little trading action going on for a particular currency pair, for example just prior to the New York close on Fridays or during news releases, dealing spreads tend to widen, sometimes by a huge margin, as a way for market makers to protect themselves when they feel that they may have to carry additional risks.

In addition to their primary role of supplying liquidity, traders from these banks also undertake intraday or short-term speculative trades based on opportunities created by their clients' transactions. Market makers usually operate a dealing desk, which refers to the market maker trading with the customer, and the presence of dealing desks means that the market maker may potentially trade against the customer. It is possible for market makers to manipulate currency prices so as to run their customers' stops or not let customers' trades reach their profit target levels. They may move their currency quotes 10-15 pips away from the interbank rates. Independent traders should always be sceptical of claims by some market makers when they say they do not operate a dealing desk.

2. Electronic Communication Networks (ECNs)

ECNs are electronic trading platforms that match buy and sell orders automatically at the specified prices. Traders tend to be more aware of their existence in stocks or futures markets.

An ECN broker gets its currency pricing from several liquidity providers such as banks, market makers or other traders who are connected to the system. When an order is placed, it is routed to the best available bid or ask price in its system.

Unlike the case of some market makers, spreads on ECNs are variable rather than fixed. Although ECN-type brokers typically charge a small commission, you can usually get tighter spreads on many currency pairs due to the large liquidity pool available. Risks of trade manipulation are also minimised when using genuine ECN brokers as compared to brokers that operate dealing desks.

How the OTC Structure Affects Self-Directed Traders

Limited access to interbank market

Individual retail traders, most of whom trade in much smaller size compared to those of banks, generally trade through forex brokers instead of directly accessing the interbank market. This aspect of OTC shifts the odds of success against individual traders, especially if the forex broker acts as a market maker. Since traders have to deal directly with their brokers, the latter will usually hold the opposite side of the transactions. If a trader is bullish on say, the USD/JPY, he or she will go long by buying a specific quantity of USD/JPY from the market maker, who will then effectively be short USD/JPY by selling to the trader. Because of the inherent conflict of interest that exists, this arrangement does not sit well with many individual traders as they fear that the market maker will trade against them, and that is not an uncommon practice in the market making industry.

No information on volume

Since buy and sell transactions are not cleared by a central system, there is no way of knowing the total volume of trade. Lack of volume data can pose a challenge to stocks or futures traders who have made the switch to currencies as they may have become used to checking volume.

No singular exchange rate at any one time

Exchange rates do differ from place to place, screen to screen, depending on which parties are offering what. Cash transactions take place between countless parties at any one time, and there is no exchange which records all these transactions.

For example, while the exchange rate of EUR/USD may show 1.2500/1.2503 on Broker X, the EUR/USD exchange rate on Broker Y may be 1.2505/1.2508 at the same time. There isn't a universal absolute exchange rate of any currency pair at any given time.

Some independent traders are not even aware of this peculiar aspect of OTC dealings. Since there can be a few different prices for a currency pair at any one time, you may not be able to see what is the best available price if you trade through only one market maker. Generally, though, the rates provided by market makers to retail traders are quite close to the pricing quoted in the interbank market.

Varying spreads

Spreads on currency pairs vary from broker to broker, with some market makers setting fixed spreads, while ECNs will have varying (usually tighter) spreads in each currency pair, depending on market liquidity. Spreads and/or commissions should preferably be calculated in advance before each trade so that you can decide where your breakeven price will be after taking into account all these business costs.

No standard data

Exchange rates differ from one market maker to another because there is no consensus specified by a centralised market. Different market makers have different rates at the same time although usually not differing by more than a few pips. A trader would have to accept what is being quoted by his broker unless he compares prices with other brokers. Price charts from different price feed vendors will also look slightly different as they each have their own data source. Although, in general, the currency prices are quite similar.

The forex trading day

Also, being a 24-hour market, boundaries of a trading day are blurred. Traders from around the world are in various time zones. Traders from, say, Singapore would display a different timing from their US counterparts – who tend to display EST (Eastern Standard Timing) on their price charts. As a result, many traders display GMT (Greenwich Mean Time) on their charts, so that a trading "day" commences and ends according to GMT.

Summary

The OTC nature of the forex market can be a bane to serious forex traders, who long for price and execution transparency – something which is standard for stock and futures markets. While the trading arena has had a boost from the CME-Reuters joint venture of a central forex exchange, it remains to be seen if that can benefit independent traders. Trade manipulation by some market-making brokers is something that is difficult for traders to prove, and something that is easy for the culprits to dismiss.

However, despite the limitations that come with the OTC territory, spot forex trading can be extremely financially rewarding for those who are aware of the limitations and know how to deal with them.

3:
How To Overcome The Odds Of Trading Forex

3: How To Overcome The Odds Of Trading Forex

It is one of the hardest jobs in the world to make big money. And trading forex is not one of the easiest ways – despite what many new traders believe. Many traders fail, and they empty their trading accounts before they learn how to exploit the forex market to their advantage. Although there are also traders who are successful in forex trading, their numbers are small compared to the majority of losers. Many times, traders are not aware that they have the power and might to shift the odds to their favour, that they can dramatically increase their chances of success if they want to. The main reason why many traders get defeated by the market can be attributed to their lack of knowledge.

In this 21st century, where the buzzword is knowledge, it is not just a matter of working hard, but also a matter of working smart. Knowledge is the key that can open many doors – if you have an intimate knowledge of how something works, you can then come up with ways to exploit what you know to your advantage. This applies to forex trading as well. Not only must you know and understand how the forex market works, you also need to understand your own emotions and other people's emotions. You need to know how to identify high probability trade setups and how to manage your money wisely.

For every transaction in the forex market, there are winners and losers. Your goal is to make more overall profits than losses over a period of time, and to emerge an overall winner. My approach to consistent trading success lies in three main pillars, or the 3Ms: Mind, Money and Method.

Mind

Out of the three Ms, I find the Mind component to be the most crucial to trading success.

It is often said that we are our own worst enemy. In forex trading, I couldn't agree more with that saying. Human beings are emotional creatures, and most of our decisions are guided more by emotions than logical thinking. Our mind is capable of playing tricks on us; we can get seduced into unfavourable situations by our emotions. Emotions can work for us or against us. Sometimes they can save us from landing in a pile of sticky mess, but sometimes they can land us in it. We can also turn the tables around by playing tricks on our mind, making it believe whatever we want it to believe. Both internal and external battles can be fought and won through the optimal harnessing of the Mind's power.

Do you have the mental strength?

A trader's mindset is the most important ingredient of success. Whether you are new to trading currencies or a forex trader who has some experience, here are some questions to ask yourself:

Do you really have a strong desire to succeed in forex trading?

Sure, every one wants to succeed in something, but do you have the desire to want to succeed in forex trading? First of all, this field is not for every one, for you must have the passion for it. If you just want to try your luck, or dabble, in trading, you will just end up among the majority who lose their money. You must have the deep desire to want to accomplish your goals, because without this desire, your thoughts will not materialise into action, and it is action that could transform your goals to reality. To be a successful trader, you must be highly self-motivated, have a concrete plan of action, and not be afraid of failure.

Are you prepared to devote a lot of time and effort into picking up trading skills and knowledge?

To be really good at anything, you need skills and knowledge in that field. A huge amount of time, effort and money is required for a trader to attain consistent success in forex trading. Despite the availability of forex trading-related resources on the internet, and in the bookstores, traders can find it quite daunting to learn about trading on their own as they do not know what there is to be known. If you do not wish to pay large tuition fees to the market, or if you wish to shorten your learning time, you may want to consider online trading courses or physical seminars on forex trading. I recommend that you check out those which are offered by skilled and practising instructors.

Note: Be wary of signing up for courses or seminars that are full of hype, for they can be very misleading. Avoid those that give you the impression that you can attain consistent profits after two days of intensive learning, or those that require you to purchase expensive software. While there are some shortcuts to gaining knowledge via courses or seminars, there is no substitute for honing your trading skills in the market.

Are you willing to accept losses as part of trading?

Every one makes mistakes, and mistakes are inevitable. Got a trading loss? Then whip out your trading log to record what your mistakes are and what you have learnt from that losing trade. Always have something positive to take away from your losses, and treat it as a learning experience. Don't dwell on your losses. Know that there will be other trades coming your way.

Are you willing to take sole responsibility for your trading decisions?

You read some market analysis, and then trade according to what the analyst is saying. That trade turns out to be a loser, and you turn around to blame it on that market report. It is too easy to shuffle blame on others, and say "It wasn't me/my fault." It is fine to read about other people's opinions about the market, but make sure that you do your own analysis of the market, which you will gradually learn to do so with confidence if you are still relatively new to forex trading. It is dangerous to blame losses on other people, the forex market, or the stars, for you are the only person responsible for pulling the trigger. And if you blame others you will never be able to find out how you can improve.

Fear and greed

Fear and greed are the two dominant emotions that affect not just the state of our mind, but also the currency market. In fact, the fluctuations of these two emotions are the main drivers of the currency market. There are, of course, other emotions that exist in the market such as disappointment, regret and so on, but fear and greed are the principal forces that tilt the scales of supply and demand of currencies. When traders feel overly optimistic about a country or its currency, they become consumed by the great hope that the currency would appreciate in value against another currency. They are then guided by this hope and greed to buy the currency pair now so that they could hopefully sell it at a higher price in the future. Greed then grows into euphoria, as traders continue to buy and buy, thus taking currency prices to newer highs. However, since currencies always move in pairs (when one currency in a pair goes up, the other goes down), fear is also an equally strong emotion that guides the currency movements. When people are buying a currency with great hope, they are also selling the other currency in the pair with great fear. On the other hand, when currency prices go down, fear and greed are also the main drivers of the move. All in all, fear and greed are behind the steering wheel of the currency market.

So, while you must learn to recognise these emotions in the market, the problem comes when you allow them to distort your logic when it comes to making trading decisions, as most of these decisions will turn out bad, and are likely to cause you to regret your actions later.

Every trader has emotions of fear and greed; there is no way you can avoid feeling these emotions, unless you want to adopt the drastic measure of removing your amygdala – which just happens to be a very important part of a human's brain. Since there is no way of banishing these emotions for good, the best thing to do is to control these emotions, instead of letting them control the way you think and act.

Face and control your fears

Since greed can be categorised as a kind of fear, which is the fear of missing out, I will discuss the primary types of fears relating to trading, and how they can be overcome.

The first step to preventing fears from ruining your trading performance is to recognise the various forms of fear that is connected to trading. And once you recognise the type of fear you are experiencing, the easier it is for you to handle that emotional obstacle so that you can trade better. That is the key to emotion-free trading. It is not about pretending that those fears do not exist, but how you handle them that matters. Here are some common trading-related fears.

Fear of missing out

Why do so many people rush to departmental store sales, or rushed to buy technology stocks during the dot-com boom? Any kind of buying mania stems from a very strong emotion that is commonly invoked in people, and that is the fear of missing out. This particular fear is also a form of greed because it makes people salivate at the prospect of a seemingly good opportunity that is "too good to pass up".

In trading, this fear manifests itself especially during a sharp rally or decline of a currency pair. For example, you may see on your screen that EUR/USD is making new highs, as it keeps going up and up. Your heart begins to pound really fast, and you have a million thoughts zipping through your brain, with most of the thoughts urging you to *buy now, now, now*. You feel the acute pain of not being in the market as EUR/USD continues to move higher. You think, "Everyone else is buying, and I haven't. I am losing out!" This fear of losing out is so strong that it then hypnotises you into frantically placing buy orders, despite your having some doubts at the far back of your mind.

The "How can I not be buying (selling) when every one else is buying (selling)" mindset is extremely dangerous, because your logical thinking faculty becomes replaced by fear, and when you trade haphazardly, it can result in huge trading losses. It has even been suggested that the fear of losing out is much stronger than the fear of losing one's entire trading account. Traders suffering from this type of fear are usually the ones who get onto a trend too late.

Be disciplined and hold off that mouse whenever you sense that this type of fear is creeping up on you. Think instead of all those traders who are pouring dumb money into the market, and be glad that you know better than them not to join in the craze.

Fear of losses

Trading is a game – there will be winners, and there will be losers. Sometimes you win some, sometimes you lose some. Losses are bound to happen, no matter how accurate a trading system may be. Losses can even occur consecutively, especially under changing market conditions or when you don't keep your monster emotions at bay.

The fear of losing is most prominent in new traders as they do not yet have adequate trading skills and knowledge to help assess and evaluate trading opportunities with a high level of confidence. This can lead to trading paralysis, whereby traders become afraid of pulling the trigger when it comes to entering or exiting trades as they fear losing money or a big portion of their trading capital.

However, if you have a reasonable stop-loss order in place, that is in accordance to your money management rules, you should have no reason of being fearful of damaging the trading account based on just one trade. That is what stop-loss orders are for – to guard against huge losses.

When you do encounter hesitancy in pulling the trigger, evaluate if you have valid reasons for doing so or if you are simply held back by fear. To overcome the fear of losing, remember that you have a reasonable stop-loss in place, and that even if that trade turns out to be an unfortunate loss, you won't suffer financially or psychologically. Traders just have to get used to the reality that losses are inevitable. The trick is to ensure that your losses are kept small so that you do not harm both your trading account and your state of mind.

Fear of making wrong decisions

Rest assured that "being able to predict the market" is not one of the prerequisites for being a successful forex trader. No one, and no computer system, can predict future currency moves with 100% accuracy. Trading is based on probability, not certainty. If you think that it is highly likely for USD/CHF to go up, you go long, and if you think there is a high chance for USD/JPY to go down, you short. A trader does not have to be right. It does not matter at all whether he or she is right or wrong; what counts is whether he or she is profitable in the long run.

Traders should not be hung up on the outcome of single trades, or even a few trades, as trading performance has to be assessed over a period of time. What matters is that you end up profitable over a period of time. Once you place less emphasis on being correct on a current trade, your fear of making wrong decisions should abate, thus enabling you to make better trading decisions without feeling burdened by the overwhelming pressure to be correct in that trade. Remember that there will be times of losses and times of profits, which is why it is so important to enter only trades that have a high probability of success.

Focus on the big picture

Do not get caught up in feeling invincible or pessimistic after a win or a loss. As trading is a very highly charged and emotional activity, it is very easy for traders to oscillate between emotional highs and lows. The outcome of just one trade should not affect your overall performance, unless you have violated proper risk management guidelines by betting the farm on a single trade or by over-leveraging.

A trade is just one of many trades. When you are wrong on one trade or several trades, try not to beat yourself up or feel regret. Instead, analyze to see where and how you could have done better in those trades or what mistakes you may have made, and record what you have learnt from them. If there was really nothing that could have been preventable, just accept that the market is unpredictable. The outcome of one or a few winning or losing trades should not be magnified. Other trades will surely come.

Money

Why is it that many profitable positions turn into losses, and winning strategies result in losses instead of profits?

I strongly believe that once a trader has honed his or her trading skills, the ultimate factor that will affect his or her overall profitability is money management skills.

Money management is all about managing the possible risks, and it is the defining factor that separates winners and losers in forex trading. Novice traders think of how much they can harvest from the market; experienced traders think of how much they can lose to the market. Many traders are so eager to trade to make big money that they completely overlook money management. Poor money management also explains why so many traders get wiped out by the market. The first goal of money management must be to ensure long-term survival in the market, because if you don't survive to trade another day, you can forget about profits altogether.

Money management is about fully optimising your trading capital. It allows you to be proactive in managing risks, and to cope with trading losses – which are part and parcel of the game. It is an essential tool to ensure that you will have more than enough to last another day in the trading game. It is possible to have a trading system that yields 90% accuracy but still end up losing if the trader does not handle his or her money and portfolio properly. No matter how good a trading system may be, there will be times when you will experience a series of losses. Success comes to those who have set down rules for money management, and have the discipline to follow them through their trading.

Preserve your capital

The shining light that attracts all traders to the forex market is the prospect of being able to grow their money by tapping into the online trading platform as their own in-house money tree. In almost any field, it is true that most people are drawn to short-term benefits, but are myopic when it comes to long-term planning. Trading is no exception.

When risk capital is put aside for trading, you are hoping that this amount of money could be transformed into a much bigger amount; otherwise, what would be the point of risking it? But if this capital runs out, what can you bank on to make your desired profits? After all, money begets money. Hence, preservation of capital is the key to ensuring a trader's long-term survival in the market, for, without survival, there can be no wealth generation.

To drive home the importance of capital preservation, I will discuss the concept of *drawdown*, and how that is relevant to money management.

Drawdown

Drawdown refers to the decline in account equity from a trade or series of trades. In other words, it is the amount of money that you lose – it is usually expressed as a percentage of your total trading equity at any given time. Drawdown is not an indication of your overall trading performance, as it is calculated when you have a losing trade against your new equity high or your original equity, depending on which is higher.

For example, you start with a trading account of $10,000, and lose $2000. Your drawdown would be 20%. Now you are left with $8000. If you subsequently gain $1000 and then lose $3000, you now have a drawdown of 40% ($8000 + $1000 - $3000 = $6000, which is 40% loss on your original equity amount of $10,000).

But let's say you do not have a losing trade, and have made $3000 on your $10,000 trading capital, so that increases your trading equity to $13,000. However, you then lose $2000 out of $13,000 on your next trade. Your drawdown would be 15% ($13,000 - $2000 = $11,000, which is a 15% decrease from the new equity high of $13,000).

An important thing to note is that a 100% drawdown will wipe out your trading account, regardless of whatever percentage you are up in your trading account.

Recovering from drawdown

As drawdown gets bigger and bigger, it becomes increasingly difficult to recover the equity. Many people are not aware that in order to recoup the percentage of equity that they lose, they will need to gain a bigger percentage just to break even. If you have lost 10% of your capital, do you think you can break even with a gain of 10%? The answer is no. It will require an 11.11% return on your new account balance for you to recoup that 10% loss. Let me show you with numbers.

Let's say, you start with an initial trading capital of $10,000 and lose $1000, which is 10% of your capital. In order to recoup that $1000 loss, you will need to make $1000 out of your $9000 remaining balance, which is equivalent to 11.11% ($1000/$9000 x 100).

OK, that is not scary yet, but if you start losing more and more of your capital (bigger and bigger drawdowns), the faster you will go down the rabbit hole. Refer to the table opposite:

% Loss of Equity	% Profit to Recoup Loss
10%	11.11%
20%	25%
30%	42.85%
40%	66.66%
50%	100%
60%	150%
70%	233%
80%	400%
90%	900%
100%	**Wiped Out**

As you can see, while losses increase arithmetically, the gains that are needed to recoup them increase geometrically.

For an 80% drawdown, can you imagine quadrupling your account just to break even?

While many traders hope for that One Big Win that will magically transform them into millionaires overnight, they are more likely to be confronted with the One Big Loss that will threaten their survival in the forex market if they do not exercise careful money management. If a trader has a big loss, he or she will have to spend more time to get back to where he or she was before, instead of using the time to make profits. Traders who burn out quickly in the market are those who do not show respect for risk. On the other hand, traders who have flourished are those who fully understand the importance of stringent money management and incorporate that into their trading approach. There is no way around to recouping slowly, unless you want to drive yourself to total destruction by risking more and more of your equity to try to make back your losses. Holding on to a losing trade for too long is the biggest cause of a big drawdown.

Be well-capitalised

Most new traders run out of money even before they see any profits in their trading account. Indeed, those who are new to trading most likely do not have a good understanding of the risks and dangers that are lurking in the market, and few even know what drawdown means or have even heard of this word. Many of them do know that trading can be very risky if they do not know what they are doing or how things work in the currency market and, to them, one of the obvious but incorrect ways to limit this risk is by allocating just a small amount of money to their trading account. They think that they should not be investing too much money into a business start-up before it starts to generate profits. There are also many new traders who begin their trading business with little initial capital as they simply do not have enough money. Whatever their reasons may be, being under-capitalised will be more than just a mistake; it is often the prelude to trading failure.

Forex traders who want to set themselves up for success must be well-capitalised. Never mind that some retail brokers are offering a minimum account deposit of just a few hundred dollars – a paltry amount that almost every one can afford. Sufficient initial capital must be available to cushion the impact of a string of consecutive losses, so that you do not wipe out your trading account. A series of losses is really not that uncommon in trading, and all traders must be financially prepared for it.

Those with insufficient trading capital tend to set really tight stops, which will naturally then lead to a higher probability of being stopped out. They also tend to have a good chunk of their account eaten away by unreasonably large losses in relation to their trading account, if they do not set tight stops. So it seems that whichever way they turn, they are setting themselves up for failure, unless they are willing to trade smaller lot sizes.

Looking outside of trading, many other businesses fail because the owners often do not have enough capital to tide them over the initial starting phase. For example, a new restaurant owner must set aside enough money to pay the rent of the restaurant for at least a few months to a few years, assuming that the restaurant would not make any net profits in that period of time. If the owner only has enough to pay for two months rent from his or her own pocket, and the restaurant is still not making enough to cover the rent and other expenses in the third month, how do you think the business is going to sustain itself? The entire business could fail, not because of the business model, but because of the lack of sufficient capital to keep the business running while the customer base builds up. Trading, as I have mentioned before, must be treated just like any other business, not a frivolous casual pursuit.

The point is this: by starting off sufficiently capitalised, you are more likely to adhere to your money management rules and, by doing so, you are really giving yourself a good fighting chance in the market. Don't cut yourself short.

Cap your losses and get your profits

Before you execute any trades, you should know where your threshold of pain is – yes, I'm referring to the pain of losses. Losses are really just part of the trading game. If trading losses are kept manageable and reasonable, they should not dent your trading account too much, provided that you are well-capitalised. Knowing when to get out of a losing position in the currency market is a very important tool of risk management. Stop-loss orders allow traders to set an exit point for a losing trade, and are the best weapon against emotional trading. While I recommend that traders place a stop-loss order at the time of placing their entry order, mental stops may also be used – but preferably by traders who are more disciplined.

Stop-loss orders should not be so tight that normal market volatility triggers the order. From experience, it is much wiser to have a wider but reasonable stop than to have an unreasonably tight stop. Generally, a stop-loss order should not be shifted in the losing direction while a position is opened.

A good trader should know beforehand when to cut his or her losses, and also when to get out of the market with profits. Profit limit orders should reflect a realistic expectation of gains based on the currency pair's trading activity and the length of time you want to hold the position for.

Method

Every one is eager to get hold of the Holy Grail, whether it truly exists or not. It is indeed the elusive factor that courts the relentless determination of its seekers. A lot of traders – both new and not so new – seek the perfect formula that is capable of predicting with 100% accuracy the future price movements. Want to know where it lies? It only exists in the creative part of the mind – together with fairies and gnomes.

There is no perfect formula or strategy that can achieve that unrealistic goal because people who are involved in the financial markets evolve with changing market circumstances, even though certain old habits die hard. Despite the non-existence of the magic formula, there are certainly high probability ways of trading the forex market. While the bulk of this book is focused on the Method part, you need to combine Method with both Money and Mind in order to attain success in the trading business.

The old question: technicals or fundamentals?

There are generally three broad categories of forex traders pertaining to what they base their trading decisions on:

1. the technical trader,

2. the fundamental trader,

3. the trader who combines both technicals and fundamentals.

Each type of trader has a distinctively different way of interpreting the currency market based on his or her own opinions.

Technical trading

A technical trader believes that historical data has a big role in the forecasting of future price action, and is thus devoted to currency price chart analysis, making use of various charting tools such as support and resistance levels, trendlines and a myriad of chart indicators to understand past price behaviour so as to predict what the market will do next.

Most forex traders employ some kind of technical analysis to help them make trading decisions. In fact, technical analysis of the forex market is so prevalent among market players that self-fulfilling prophecies often occur at price levels where people's responses become quite predictable; that is, you will know if most players will buy or sell at those levels due to their historical significance. Technical traders assume that everything that is to be known about the market has already been factored into the current price.

Fundamentals trading

The second category is the fundamental trader who weighs and analyzes the various economic news and information relating to the country of a particular currency in order to come up with a fair evaluation of the value of that currency relative to another. Fundamental traders believe that the exchange rate of currencies are largely driven by economic and geopolitical conditions, aside from central bank interventions, and will keep track of economic data such as trade balances, inflation, Gross Domestic Product (GDP), unemployment rates, interest rates and so on. They are also concerned about what policymakers have to say regarding the monetary policy of the country, and will keep on top of these when speeches are scheduled.

Combining technicals and fundamentals

Since there are advantages of analyzing the forex market from these two different fields, it would be too restrictive to just side with one area and ignore the other. The most effective traders tend to make trading decisions based on a combination of both technical and fundamental factors in order to get a feel of the overall market sentiment, and then decide to either trade that sentiment or to trade against it taking a contrarian approach.

The strategies taught in this book must always be combined with the prevailing market sentiment, which is influenced mainly by fundamentals.

Method is malleable

I believe that an important factor of trading success lies in the matching of Method with the trader's own personality and trading style. Some strategies may work well for some traders, but may not have the same results for others over a period of time. This may seem puzzling for some people who are wondering that if something works for someone, then it should work for other people as well. In trading, there are so many other factors specific to each trader that can influence the overall trading performance – his or her emotions, psychology, trading time frame, money management rules, lifestyle, trading capital and so on.

The strategies included in this book are open to customisation according to your own personal preference. While most of the strategies are meant for day or swing trading, you have the freedom to adjust certain parameters to suit your own trading time frame and/or other preferences.

Summary

If you build your trading foundation on the 3Ms of Mind, Money and Method, your odds of achieving consistent success in the forex market will be higher than if you were to focus on just the Method. Many traders do not give themselves the fighting chance and time to stay in the game as they are prone to getting wiped out very quickly.

4:
The Ten Rules
For Forex Trading

4. The Ten Rules For Forex Trading

I list here ten rules that I think are important for trading forex. I have split the list into five Dos and five Don'ts.

Dos

1. When trying out a new trading strategy, always test it in a demo account, or with a small amount of money, before you commit more money to it.

2. Always keep a record of each of your trades, with details of: why you got in, how you got out and why it turned out the way it did.

3. Have a personalised trading plan and update it as you learn from the market.

4. If you are unsure of a trade, stay out. It is better to miss an opportunity than to have a loss.

5. When trading, keep up-to-date with both the fundamentals and technicals affecting the market. A trader in the dark is a trader in the red.

Don'ts

1. Don't trade with money you can't afford to lose! It will affect you emotionally, and you will most likely lose it to irrational trading.

2. Don't follow someone else's trading advice blindly. Always know why you are getting into a trade, and how you are going to get out of it.

3. Don't be concerned about being right. Just be concerned about being profitable.

4. Don't over-leverage. Chances are that your account will be decimated before you can recoup your losses and go into profit.

5. Don't revenge-trade the market. Vent your frustrations elsewhere after a loss.

STRATEGIES

5:
Strategy 1 –
Market Sentiment

Strategy 1 – Market Sentiment

How do you view the forex market?

Do you see it as a big mechanical matrix which is devoid of emotions? Or do you think of it in mathematical and probability terms? Perhaps, you may even view it as just a vast network of computers which are designed to cheat the trader sitting in front of his or her computer and trading electronically. Most traders I know have a love-hate relationship with the forex market, thinking that the market is, in turn, either against them or for them.

To me, the forex market is nothing more than the compressed display of emotions at any one time emanating from currency speculators around the world. It is similar to a big living organism, like a human being, which is made up of numerous cells, with each cell carrying out its own function and interacting with other cells of the body, working to keep the body alive with round-the-clock chemical and biological processes.

The forex market is alive as a macro living organism, which comprises a vast number of market participants acting out their perceptions and emotions, thus driving the blood around the invisible entity. The participation of each player, whether the player is an institutional dealer or an independent trader, is akin to the individual functioning of a cell, which collectively will constitute the whole organism – the forex market in this case. Knowing what the market thinks and how it thinks is crucial to trading success because, ultimately, the trader is dealing with other traders out there, and needs to know what they are thinking. Even if you see the market as an enemy, what could be better than knowing the weak points and being able to read the mind of your adversary?

In this chapter, I shall focus on how you can better understand the market, and use that knowledge as one of your trading weapons.

What Is Market Sentiment?

Market sentiment is simply what the majority of the market is perceived to be thinking or feeling about the market – it is the most important factor that drives the currency market.

This is so because traders tend to act based on what they feel and think of certain currencies, regarding their strength or weakness relative to other currencies. I will assume that when you trade currencies, you don't blindfold yourself to simply pick any pair to buy or sell, leaving it to randomness to determine your profit/loss statement at the end of the day or month.

Market sentiment sums up the overall dominating emotion of the majority of the market participants, and explains the current actions of the market, as well as the future course of actions of the market. The trend adopted by the forex market is actually a reflection of the current market sentiment, which in turn guides the trading decisions of other traders, whether they should long or short a currency pair. In the process of making educated trading decisions, traders have to weigh a multitude of factors which could influence the bias of a currency, before making up their minds about the current and future state of certain currencies. One thing to note is that market sentiment is not logical; it is primarily based on traders' emotions, which is really one of the greatest, if not the greatest, factor in the determination of a currency exchange rate.

There are three main types of sentiment when it comes to forming opinions in the forex market:

1. bullish,

2. bearish or

3. just plain confused.

If the majority of the market wants to sell that currency, the market sentiment is deemed to be bearish; if the majority wants to buy that currency, the market sentiment is bullish; and when most market participants are unsure of what to do at the moment, the sentiment ends up being mixed. Since the US dollar is the currency on the opposite side of 80% of all foreign exchange transactions, most traders will be concerned with what the market thinks about the US dollar. Currency prices simply embody the market's perceptions of reality and the sum total of traders' emotions.

Market sentiment acts like a fickle lover, capable of changing its mind based on certain incoming new information which can upset the existing sentiment. One moment everyone could be buying the US dollar in anticipation of a stronger dollar; the next second they could all be dumping it as they fear the dollar would start to weaken due to the impact of some new piece of information, which is almost always some fundamental news.

Understanding the current market sentiment and exploiting it appropriately with the other strategies discussed in this book can help maximise your trading profits, because if you can guess what the other market players are thinking about, and understand why the market is doing what it is doing, you will be in a better position to plan your entry and exit points and timing.

What Factors Influence Market Sentiment?

Interest rates

Trends in interest rates are one of the most significant factors influencing market sentiment, as interest rates play a huge role affecting the supply and demand of currencies.

Every currency in the world has interest rates attached to them, and these rates are decided by central banks. For example, the Fed in the US determines the country's interest rates; the Bank of Japan (BOJ) sets Japan's interest rates; the Reserve Bank of New Zealand (RBNZ) decides on New Zealand's interest rates and so on. Some currencies have higher interest rates than others, and these are usually the currencies that attract the most attention from savvy international investors who are always looking across the global landscape in the continual search for a better interest rate yield on fixed-income investments. This, of course, also depends on the geopolitical or economic risks of that particular currency. Just like when a bank lends money to a higher-risk borrower, high-risk currencies require a significantly higher interest rate for investors to consider keeping money in those currencies.

What causes fluctuations in interest rates?

The value of money can and does decrease when there is an upward revision of prices of most goods and services in a country. Generally, when a country's economy expands or when energy costs go up, goods ranging from clothing, food to computers, and services ranging from public transport to spa treatments get more expensive, thus eroding the value of money. The nice word for this erosion in value is, of course, *inflation*.

Controlling inflation

Central banks are responsible for ensuring price stability in their own country, and one of the ways they employ to fight inflationary pressures is through the setting of interest rates. If inflation risks are seen to be edging upward in, say, the US, the Fed would raise the federal funds rate, which is the rate at which banks charge each other for overnight loans. When the overnight rate is changed, retail banks will change their prime lending rates accordingly, hence affecting businesses and individuals. An increase in interest rates is an attempt to make money more expensive to borrow so that there will be a gradual decrease in demand for that currency, thus slowing down an overheated economy. The opposite scenario is true too: when a country faces deflation, or even decreased inflation, which is often the result of decreased spending, whether by the government, consumers or investors, it prompts the central bank to lower interest rates so as to stimulate spending.

Interest rates and currencies

The most important way in which interest rates can influence currency prices is through the widespread practice of the *carry trade*.

A carry trade involves the borrowing and subsequent selling of a certain currency with a relatively low interest rate, then using the funds to buy a currency which gives a higher interest rate, in an attempt to gain the difference between these two rates – which is known as the *interest rate differential*. The trader is paid interest on the currency he or she is long in, and must pay interest on the currency he or she is shorting. This difference is the *cost of carry*. Therefore, a currency with a higher interest rate tends to be highly sought after by investors looking for a higher return on their investments.

Rising interest rates in a country tends to strengthen that country's currency relative to other currencies as investors exchange other currencies to buy the currency of that country when they transfer their assets into the country with the higher interest rates. The increased demand for that particular currency will thus push up the currency price against other currencies.

For instance, in 2005 there was a strong interest among Japanese investors to invest in New Zealand dollar-denominated assets due to rising interest rates in New Zealand. The then near-zero interest rates in Japan forced a lot of Japanese investors to look outside of their country for better yields on cash deposits or fixed-income instruments. (See Figure 5.1)

Figure 5.1: New Zealand Dollar/Japanese Yen (Nov 2004 – Dec 2005)

The New Zealand dollar rose in value against the Japanese yen in 2005 as a result of massive cross-border shifting of assets.

When forex traders anticipate this kind of situation, they become more inclined to buy that high-interest-rate currency as well, knowing that there is likely to be massive buying interest for that currency.

For example, if the Fed announces a series of interest rate hikes in the US, whereas the Bank of Japan has no intention to raise rates in Japan, there is bound to be more buying interest for USD/JPY, thus pushing up the US dollar against the Japanese yen, and even possibly against other currencies as well. This situation occurred in 2005, which caused USD/JPY to rally around 1900 pips from the start of the year to December 2005, as you can see from Figure 5.2. This divergence in monetary policy between the US and Japan had created a very bullish US dollar sentiment in the market, attracting more and more traders to long USD/JPY.

Figure 5.2: US Dollar/Japanese Yen (Nov 2004 – Dec 2005)

The US dollar strengthened against the Japanese yen in 2005 as a result of a divergence in the monetary policies of the US and Japan.

So, in general, rising interest rates in a country should boost the market sentiment regarding the currency of that country.

The opposite is true too: when interest rates are cut in a country, that would result in quite a bearish sentiment regarding the currency of that country, and traders would be more willing to sell than buy that particular currency.

Economic growth

Besides interest rates, economic growth of countries can also have a big impact on the overall currency market sentiment.

Since the United States has the largest economy in the world, the US economy is a key factor in determining the overall market sentiment, especially of currency pairs that have the USD component. A robust economic expansion, coupled with a healthy labour market, tends to boost consumer spending in that country, and this helps companies and businesses to flourish. A country with a strong economy is in a better position to attract more overseas investments into the country, as investors generally prefer to invest in a solid economy that is growing at a steady pace.

Investments pouring into a country requires the currency of that country to be bought in exchange of other currencies; this increased demand for that country's currency should cause that currency to strengthen against other currencies. Forex traders, expecting this consequence, will put on their bullish cap to buy that currency before the investors do.

Some of the most important indicators of a country's economic growth include:

1. Gross Domestic Product (GDP),

2. the unemployment rate, and

3. trade balance data.

These are explained below.

1. GDP

The GDP measures the total value of all goods and services that are originated from the country; the GDP figure indicates the rate of the country's expansion or contraction based on output and growth. A healthy GDP figure usually adds bullish sentiment to the currency of that country, especially if it exceeds the market's expectations.

2. Unemployment rate

The unemployment data reports the state of the labour market of a country. The lower the unemployment rate, the more positive it is for the country's economy, and hence its currency, as consumers would feel more confident about spending if they have jobs, and that would eventually impact on companies and businesses in the country, generating more output.

3. Trade balance data

Another widely watched economic indicator is the trade balance data. Trade balance measures the difference between the value of imports and exports of goods and services of a country. If a country exports more than it imports, it has a trade surplus. If imports exceed exports, then the country will end up with a trade deficit, which does not bode well for that country's currency because that currency has to be sold to buy other foreign currencies in order to pay for those imported goods and services.

For example, if the US imports an increased amount of goods and services from Europe, US dollars will have to be sold in exchange to buy euros to pay for those imports. The resulting outflow of US dollars from the United States could potentially cause a depreciation of the US dollar against the euro or other currencies, and that can affect market sentiment surrounding the USD. The opposite scenario is true for a country that is experiencing a trade surplus. However, market sentiment of a currency can still be bullish despite that country having a trade deficit, as the net amount of trade deficit could be covered by an equivalent or greater amount of capital investment pouring into that country, and thus would not be a cause for concern.

Geopolitical risks

Geopolitical risk refers to the risk of a country's foreign or domestic policy affecting domestic social and political stability in another country or regional zone.

Global geopolitical uncertainties such as terrorism, transitional change of government or nuclear threats can cause investors to lose faith in some particular currencies, and they may prefer to shift their assets into a safe haven currency when these circumstances arise. Market sentiment is very sensitive to such geopolitical developments, and can cause a strong bias towards a particular currency.

For example, during periods of high tension in the Middle East in 2006, the market formed a very bullish sentiment towards the US dollar, which became the preferred currency to hold in such turbulent times, replacing the traditional status of the Swiss franc as the safe haven currency. Forex traders should be keenly aware of the current geopolitical environment in order to keep track of any potential change in market sentiment, which could impact currency prices.

Ways of Measuring Market Sentiment

The mood of the market depends mainly on what the majority of traders think about the current market situation. But how can you get an idea of the overall sentiment of the market? You can do so by reading reports by analysts and financial journalists in news wires or by visiting online trading forums to see what other traders are discussing. However, these ways of getting a feel of the current market sentiment are not too accurate; you may think that other traders are in a buying or selling mood, but that may not be what is really happening in reality. Here are some of the more effective ways of gauging market sentiment:

1. The Commitment of Traders (COT) report

2. The market's reactions to news releases

These are explained in more details below.

1. Commitment Of Traders (COT) report

What is the COT?

The COT report provides traders with detailed positioning information about the futures market, and is, in my opinion, one of the most underrated tools that forex traders can make use of to enhance their trading performance.

The report is compiled and released weekly by the Commodity Futures Trading Commission (CFTC) in the United States every Friday at 15:30 Eastern Time, and records open interest information about the futures market based on the previous Tuesday. Anyone can access the COT report for free on the CFTC website (www.cftc.gov/cftc/cftccotreports.htm).

There are basically two types of reports available: the futures-only COT report and the futures-and-options-combined COT report. I usually just access the futures-only report for a glimpse of what has happened in the futures dimension of the forex market. In order to get through to the currency futures data, you have to wade past other commodities like milk, feeder cattle and so on, so a little patience is required.

Even though the data arrives three days late, the information nonetheless can be helpful since many traders spend their weekend analyzing the COT report. The time lag between reporting and release is the main handicap of the COT data, but despite this limitation, you can still use it as a sentiment tool.

Figure 5.3 shows a page from the December 19, 2006, COT report (short format), displaying data for the Chicago Mercantile Exchange's Euro FX futures contract. You can see the long and short positions held by traders in each of the three main categories defined by the CFTC, as explained below.

Figure 5.3: sample COT report

```
EURO FX - CHICAGO MERCANTILE EXCHANGE                         Code-099741
FUTURES ONLY POSITIONS AS OF 12/19/06                    |
------------------------------------------------------------| NONREPORTABLE
     NON-COMMERCIAL        |    COMMERCIAL    |    TOTAL     | POSITIONS
------------------------|------------------|------------------|----------------
  LONG  | SHORT  |SPREADS |  LONG  | SHORT  |  LONG  | SHORT  |  LONG  | SHORT
---------------------------------------------------------------------------
(CONTRACTS OF 125,000 EUROS)                       OPEN INTEREST:     194,079
COMMITMENTS
 110,993  19,023    1,521   19,007 144,006 131,521 164,550   62,558   29,529

CHANGES FROM 12/12/06 (CHANGE IN OPEN INTEREST:    -36,166)
  -1,195    3,518   -4,368 -27,466 -31,711 -33,029 -32,561   -3,137   -3,605

PERCENT OF OPEN INTEREST FOR EACH CATEGORY OF TRADERS
    57.2      9.8      0.8     9.8    74.2    67.8     84.8     32.2     15.2

NUMBER OF TRADERS IN EACH CATEGORY (TOTAL TRADERS:       128)
     68       22       12      23      22      95       53
```

COT data showing Euro FX futures positions as of December 19, 2006.

Some notes to the figure above.

- **Commercial**
  This group consists of market participants who use the futures contracts for hedging purposes, and these commercial participants are generally exporters and importers who are hedging against currency fluctuations. For example, a German car-maker, who exports to the US, expects to receive 10 million euros worth of sales within the next quarter. To hedge against the possibility of a US dollar decline which would affect the amount of euros it would receive once converted, the German car-maker would short 10 million in Euro FX futures. On the other hand, if a US car manufacturer exports 10 million US dollars worth of cars within the next quarter, it would long the equivalent in Euro FX futures contracts.

- **Non-commercial**
  This group consists of large speculators such as hedge funds, banks and so on who use currency futures just for speculation.

- **Non-reportable**
  This group consists of small speculators like retail traders.

The COT report tells you the long and short positions undertaken by participants from each category. When it comes to analyzing information pertaining to currency futures in the COT report, it is generally more relevant for traders to focus on the non-commercial participants rather than on the commercial participants. The reason behind this is that these large speculators trade the futures contracts mainly for profits, and do not have the intention to take delivery of the underlying asset, which in this case would be cash. On the other hand, commercial participants tend to maintain and roll over the same amount of contracts from month to month for hedging purposes even though these positions could be in losses. Large speculators, however, will usually close their losing positions instead of rolling them over to the next month.

Why use The COT?

The COT report allows you to gauge market sentiment in the currency futures market, which also influences the spot forex market. Currency futures are basically spot prices which are adjusted by the forwards (derived by interest rate differentials) to arrive at a future delivery price. Unlike spot forex which does not have a centralised exchange at the time of writing, currency futures are cleared at the Chicago Mercantile Exchange.

Price quotation

One of the many differences between spot forex and currency futures lies in their quoting convention. In the currency futures market, currency futures are mostly quoted as the foreign currency directly against the US dollar. For example, Swiss francs are quoted versus the US dollar in futures, unlike the USD/CHF notation in the spot forex market. So if the Swiss franc falls in value against the US dollar, USD/CHF will rise, and the Swiss franc futures will fall. On the other hand, EUR/USD in spot forex is quoted in the same way as Euro futures, so if the Euro appreciates in value, Euro futures will rise just like EUR/USD will go up.

That said, spot forex and currency futures do have one similarity: the spot and futures prices of a currency tend to move in tandem. When either the spot or futures price of a currency rises, the other also tends to rise, and when either falls, the other also tends to fall. For example, if the GBP futures price goes up, spot GBP/USD goes up (because GBP gains in strength). However, if the CHF futures price goes up, spot USD/CHF goes down (because CHF gains in strength), as both the spot and futures prices of CHF move in tandem.

Using extreme positioning

In the COT report, under each type of currency futures, you can see that the total contract volume in each category is split up between "long", "short" and "spreads", of which the first two are relevant to our analysis. What is of concern to us is whether the non-commercials are net long or short in that currency futures.

In order to determine the volume of contracts that these large speculators are holding net long or short positions of for that particular currency futures, you just need to calculate the difference between the longs and shorts, that is, subtract the number of short contracts from the number of long contracts. A positive figure shows the number of net long contracts, while a negative figure shows the number of net short contracts.

As you can see in Figure 5.4, the open interest for GBP futures on Tuesday December 19, 2006, was 149,800 contracts which was a decrease of 31,780 contracts from the previous week. The non-commercials are long 98,434 contracts and short 12,836 contracts. Therefore, they are overall net long 85,598 contracts (98434 - 12836).

Figure 5.4: sample COT report

```
BRITISH POUND STERLING - CHICAGO MERCANTILE EXCHANGE               Code-096742
FUTURES ONLY POSITIONS AS OF 12/19/06                    |
-----------------------------------------------------------| NONREPORTABLE
        NON-COMMERCIAL        |   COMMERCIAL    |    TOTAL     |   POSITIONS
-------------------------|-----------------|---------------|----------------
  LONG  | SHORT  |SPREADS |  LONG  | SHORT  |  LONG  | SHORT  |  LONG  | SHORT
-----------------------------------------------------------------------------
(CONTRACTS OF 62,500 POUNDS STERLING)                OPEN INTEREST:      149,800
COMMITMENTS
 98,434   12,836       342   18,196  121,133  116,972  134,311   32,828   15,489

CHANGES FROM 12/12/06 (CHANGE IN OPEN INTEREST:    -31,780)
 -5,327  -11,756   -2,709  -20,646  -15,842  -28,682  -30,307   -3,098   -1,473

PERCENT OF OPEN INTEREST FOR EACH CATEGORY OF TRADERS
    65.7       8.6      0.2     12.1     80.9     78.1      89.7     21.9     10.3

NUMBER OF TRADERS IN EACH CATEGORY (TOTAL TRADERS:       81)
      39       15        1       10       19       50       34
```

COT data showing British Pound futures positions as of December 19, 2006.

Usually, when a particular currency is trending up against the US dollar, the non-commercials tend to register a net long position since these large speculators tend to ride on the existing trend. The opposite situation is true too: the non-commercials tend to register a net short position when a particular currency is trending down against the US dollar. Knowing whether this category has been net long or short a few days ago only indicates to us the positioning in retrospect; this information is only useful if you compare the latest net positioning with the positioning figures from the past few weeks or months.

By comparing the latest net positioning with that of the past few weeks or months, you can tell if the latest net long or net short positioning is skewing towards an extreme reading. My observation of the financial markets is that dramatic price moves, usually at major turning points, tend to occur when the majority of the market is positioned incorrectly. And since the large speculators are more inclined to close their losing positions than the commercial hedgers, it is beneficial for us to keep an eye on their net directional positioning as well as their net contract volume in the currency futures market. If these large non-commercials are positioned on the wrong side of the market, you can expect liquidation of these positions, with the extent of liquidation depending on the total volume of contracts traded in the wrong direction.

For example, if these large funds are holding large (extreme) net long GBP positions, but GBP is declining against the US dollar due to some external catalysts like news, they will eventually have to close their longs when their stops are triggered, or decide to close their longs before getting stopped out and switch to shorting GBP on the way down. Such mass unwinding of positions tends to bring about a powerful price move in the opposite direction which could last for a few days, and it is this turning point that you could detect with the COT data before the reversal scene actually plays out.

Example: COT – using extreme position

An example of this was played out in the week through November 13-17, 2006. The COT report that was released on November 10 showed that, as of the previous Tuesday on November 7, large speculative funds upped their net GBP longs to a multi-year high of +84,280 contracts, a figure which clearly shows up as an extreme positioning on the chart as shown in Figure 5.5.

In this case, all those who had the intention to go long on GBP had already done so. As a result of this extreme net speculative positioning of GBP longs on the CME, GBP/USD in the spot market proceeded to decline by more than 300 pips in the following week through November 13-17, 2006 (Figure 5.6).

Figure 5.5: COT report for GBP/USD

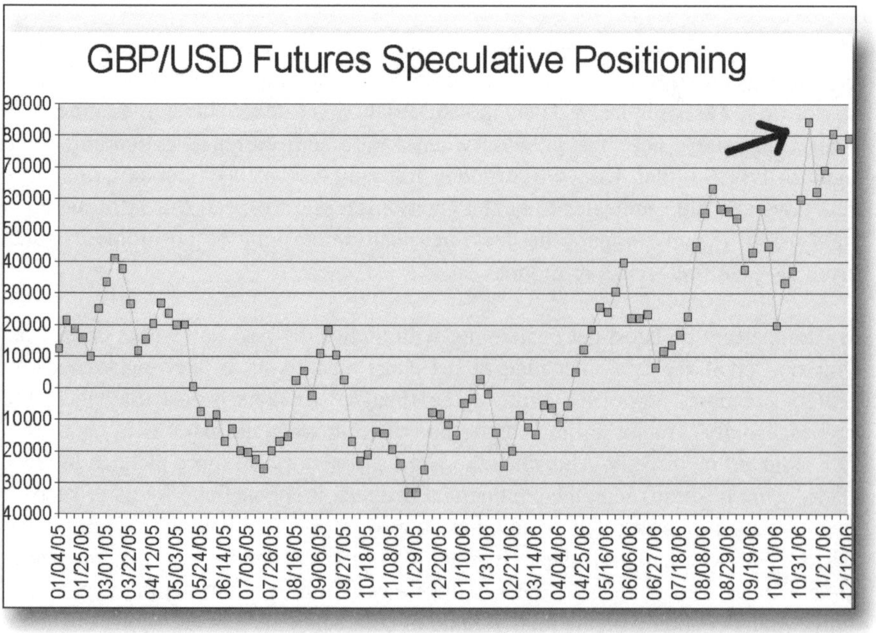

This chart shows the net speculative (*non-commercial*) positions in GBP futures on the CME. X-axis displays the dates for every three weeks even though the data for every week is shown on the chart. Y-axis displays the net number of speculative contracts. Positive numbers indicate net long positioning, while negative numbers indicate net short positioning.

Figure 5.6: extreme position leading to a fall in GBP/USD

In the week following the extreme net long speculative positioning, reflected by the COT data, GBP/USD fell by 310 pips as seen on this 60-min chart.

The presence of an extreme reading allows you to be prepared for a possible trend reversal which could occur when large speculators liquidate their positions. A mere increase or decrease of contracts for a particular currency futures does not indicate anything which could be of predictive value, as it simply shows you what has happened, but not what could possibly happen in a high-probability scenario.

COT data is a diamond in the rough

What deters many traders from using the COT report is its raw organisation of data, but that is not good enough an excuse to completely neglect this little treasure trove. The information from the COT report can be transferred into a spreadsheet so that further analysis can be conducted in a more suitable format.

The COT data itself is not sufficient to generate entry or exit signals, as the report does not consist of currency price data, but it can generate warning signals of a possible turn ahead in the spot forex market, and can be used to optimise other trading strategies you may have so that maximum profits can be reaped from the market. Analysis of the COT report does not always throw up trading opportunities in the spot forex market, but when it does, you will be better prepared for a potential turn of tide, and be more confident in your trades. Even though entries and exits cannot be timed solely based on the COT data, it can be an extremely useful tool to have in your toolbox to gauge the overall market sentiment.

2. Market's reactions to news

Another way for traders to gauge the market sentiment is by analyzing how the market responds to unanticipated news.

The forex market is very efficient at discounting future expectations by incorporating them into current prices. Very often, when news comes out better than is expected by economists and analysts, the currency of that country is more likely to soar against another currency. When the news is worse than expected, that currency is more likely to fall against another currency.

However, if the news or data turn out to be worse than expected and still the currency price soars, that is, the market reacts in a very bullish way to worse than expected data, a bright red flag should be waving at you. The opposite situation also applies: if price action remains very bearish to much better than expected news, it signals a highly suspect price move.

In short, you should look out for a contrarian market reaction to better or worse than expected news. Under these circumstances, it is better to assume that the price move is hardly supported by substance, and could reverse sometime soon. A bullish price move that is not accompanied by evidence will soon be due for a reality check, just like a bearish price move that is not accompanied by evidence is very likely to be corrected very soon. If you day trade the forex market, you may judge the market's reaction based on one piece of news, but if you position trade, monitor the market's reactions to several news to see if the responses are still contrary.

For example, if a piece of news turns out to be worse than expected, and assuming that there are no pre-release rumours or leaks of the news, and the currency pair rallies to break above a significant resistance level, you have reasons to suspect that the breakout move is likely to be false and unsustainable. Even if the currency pair manages to make new highs later on, you should be prepared for a possible trend reversal very soon. Monitoring the market's reactions to news can enable traders to identify corrective moves in the forex market.

Not all news items get the same amount of attention from big market players; news relating to the job or housing market usually get more attention. The relative significance of news will vary from time to time.

Summary

As you have seen, market sentiment can be used, and should be used, to time your trade and identify profitable trading conditions. The Market Sentiment Strategy has to be applied in conjunction with other strategies as it does not have precise entry and exit signals. By making use of information on the net speculative positioning of currency futures and by observing the market's reactions to news, you will be better equipped to gauge the market sentiment and will be able to use that extra edge to help you see what is actually happening or is going to happen in the spot forex market. Once you get a sense of the current market sentiment, you can then decide whether it is best to trade with or against the sentiment, taking into account all other factors.

While it may be sensible to trade in the direction of the current sentiment, sometimes, trading against the sentiment can also be a profitable strategy, provided that you have valid reasons to do so. For example, when the COT report indicates extreme positioning of the market, or when the market seems to be feeding off false euphoria on worse than expected news, it may be better to trade against the overall sentiment. You should, however, wait for a more precise signal that the current sentiment is wearing off before going against it, as sometimes false euphoria can last for quite some time before resulting in a reversal. This signal could be a failed breakout of some sort or some other pattern failure.

Always keep in mind that currency prices are, after all, the expressed perceptions of traders and market sentiment is really the blood that drives the market on the whole. Using the Market Sentiment Strategy can help you identify the "what" (whether to go long or short of a currency); while technical analysis shows you the "when" by helping to pinpoint the price you should enter or exit your positions.

6:
Strategy 2 –
Trend Riding

Strategy 2 – Trend Riding

Who doesn't like a trend?

Many traders live by the often-repeated "the trend is your friend until the end" rule; they are comforted with the knowledge that they are with the majority of the market. Being able to ride on a trend is akin to making full use of the wind direction to steer your ship towards your destination. For a ship to go against the wind requires a tremendous amount of effort – one has to fight the stubborn resistance from the opposing wind. Indeed, for most of the time, it pays more to be on the side of the current trend than to go against it. In the forex market, trend riders can capture any trend regardless of whether it is rising or falling in an attempt to generate trading profits.

Forex tends to have quite trending markets, regardless of which time frame you are looking at – trends are often formed on hourly, daily or weekly charts. This is due to the fact that currency price movements are very much influenced by the underlying macroeconomic factors which in turn shape the market players' views of where currency prices should be heading. With trends possibly having a long lifespan stretching to months, or even years, it is no wonder that many traders and fund managers exalt the strategy of hitching onto trends, with the glorious aim of capturing enormous profits from start to finish.

Trend riding is one of my favourite trading approaches, and I often ride the uptrend or downtrend after the trend has been established, rather than anticipating the move before it happens. I would say that even though the trend is your friend most of the times, one has to use a variety of methods to distinguish between a continuation of the trend and a possible trend reversal. But before you can ride on trends, you first need to identify what the current trend is, and to determine the time frame of the trend.

Time Frames of Trends

Sometimes, people ask me for my opinion on the current trend for certain currency pairs, I reply with another question in return, "According to the past 5 mins, 5 hours, 5 days or 5 weeks?" Some traders are not aware that different trends exist in different time frames. The question of what kind of trend is in place cannot be separated from the time frame that a trend is in. Trends are, after all, used to determine the relative direction of prices in a market over different time periods.

There are mainly three types of trends in terms of time measurement:

1. primary (long-term),

2. intermediate (medium-term), and

3. short-term.

These are discussed in further detail below.

1. Primary trend

A primary trend lasts the longest period of time, and its lifespan may range between eight months and two years. This is the major trend that can be spotted easily on longer term charts such as the daily, weekly or monthly charts. Long-term traders who trade according to the primary trend are the most concerned about the fundamental picture of the currency pairs that they are trading, since fundamental factors will provide these traders with an idea of supply and demand on a bigger scale.

2. Intermediate trend

Within a primary trend, there will be counter-cyclical trends, and such price movements form the intermediate trend. This type of trend could last from a month to as long as eight months. Knowing what the intermediate trend is of great importance to the position trader who tends to hold positions for several weeks or months at one go.

3. Short-term trend

A short-term trend can last for a few days to as long as a month. It appears during the course of the intermediate trend due to global capital flows reacting to daily economic news and political situations. Day traders are concerned with spotting and identifying short-term trends and as such short-term price movements are aplenty in the currency market, and can provide significant profit opportunities within a very short period of time.

No matter which time frame you may trade, it is vital to monitor and identify the primary trend, the intermediate trend, and the short-term trend for a better overall picture of the trend.

Trend Directions

In order to adopt the Trend Riding Strategy, you must first identify a trend direction.

You can easily gauge the direction of a trend by looking at the price chart of a currency pair. A trend can be defined as a series of higher lows and higher highs in an uptrend, and a series of lower highs and lower lows in a downtrend. In reality, prices do not always go higher in an uptrend, but still tend to bounce off areas of support, just like prices do not always make lower lows in a downtrend, but still tend to bounce off areas of resistance.

There are three trend directions a currency pair could take:

1. uptrend,

2. downtrend or

3. sideways.

1. Uptrend

In an uptrend, the base currency (which is the first currency symbol in a pair) appreciates in value. For example, if EUR/USD is in an uptrend, it means that EUR is rising higher against the USD. An uptrend is characterised by a series of higher highs and higher lows. However in real life, sometimes the currency does not make higher highs, but still makes higher lows. Base currency bulls (henceforth referred to simply as "bulls") take charge during an uptrend, taking the opportunities to bid up the base currency whenever it goes a bit lower, believing that there will be more buyers at every step, hence pushing up the prices.

2. Downtrend

On the other hand, in a downtrend, the base currency depreciates in value. For example, if EUR/USD is in a downtrend, it means that EUR is declining against the USD. A downtrend is characterised by a series of lower highs and lower lows, but similarly, the currency does not always make lower lows, but still tends to make lower highs. The downward slope of lower highs is formed by the base currency bears (will simply be known now as just "bears") who take control during a downtrend, taking every opportunity to sell because they believe that the base currency would go down even more.

3. Sideways trend

If a currency pair does not go much higher or much lower, we can say that it is going sideways. When this happens the prices are moving within a narrow range, and are neither appreciating nor depreciating much in value. If you want to ride on a trend, this directionless mode is one that you do not wish to be stuck in, for it is very likely to have a net loss position in a sideways market especially if the trade has not made enough pips to cover the spread commission costs.

For the Trend Riding Strategy, I shall focus only on the uptrend and the downtrend.

Stages of a Trend

A trend has a start point and an end point; in between these two points, the trend can exhibit different behaviours. As a trend rider, it is important to note the various stages of a trend so that you don't get on the trend train at the last stage, just when smart people are starting to disembark from it. The stages of a trend are not clear-cut, and that includes the starting and ending stages; and each stage can vary in length of time.

Let's take a look at the different stages of a trend (See Figure 6.1).

1. Nascent trend

2. Fully charged trend

3. Aging trend

4. End of trend

Figure 6.1: stages of a trend

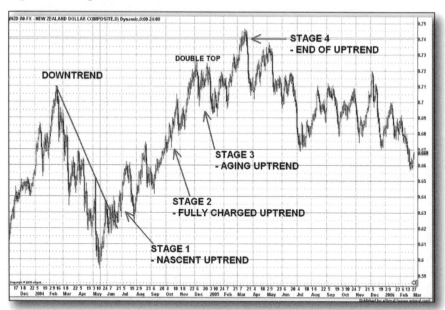

The four stages of a trend are depicted on this daily chart of NZD/USD. As you can see, Stage 1 of the uptrend started when the currency pair first emerged from the down trendline. The uptrend was confirmed at Stage 2, when NZD/USD began making higher highs and higher lows – typically characteristic of an uptrend. Later, a double top formation hinted that the uptrend was at Stage 3 when the trend was beginning to show signs of weariness. NZD/USD then made one last attempt to make a new high which failed to attract any sustained buying interest, thus paving the way for Stage 4, which signalled the end of the uptrend.

Stage 1: Nascent trend

Right after a reversal, the embryonic trend emerges into the new territory with the greatest amount of uncertainty, as traders have the least amount of confidence in the direction of the nascent trend. Price moves are often sharp, and may even retest the price levels seen before the entry into the new territory as bulls and bears wrestle for power. This characterises Stage 1 of a trend, and it is where aggressive traders get into the currency market, hoping to be right about the new direction of the trend and reap potentially the most profits by getting in early. Since this stage of the trend has the greatest level of uncertainty, it is also where the risk of trend failure is greatest.

Stage 2: Fully charged trend

By the time the trend reaches Stage 2, it is fully charged. Either the bulls or the bears have won the battle over the other by now, and are persistently pushing the currency prices higher during an uptrend, or lower during a downtrend. The highly confident behaviour of the bulls in the uptrend and of the bears in the downtrend gives little room for uncertainty about the trend direction. This stage is ideally the best time for the risk-averse trader to join in the prevailing trend, after getting confirmation from the technical picture and market sentiment.

Stage 3: Aging trend

As with human beings, a trend gets old and tired eventually. Aging of a trend typically occurs in Stage 3, and it is at this stage that you can witness the fallacies of man. Overly eager traders, especially those who have missed out on the initial stages of the trend, are now realising their tardiness, and are hopping onto the trend bandwagon, hoping to still be able to get a piece of the action. The more experienced traders are more than happy to pass on the closing legs of their transactions over to these inexperienced traders as they try to take their profits while the trend is near the peak of an uptrend, or near the bottom of a downtrend. Seasoned traders begin to lose their confidence in the strength of the trend, whereas inexperienced traders who are still hoping to gain more profits remain optimistic about the trend. So there is a mix of waning confidence and overconfidence in the trend at this stage. More price consolidation periods could be seen at this stage, and chart patterns like head-and-shoulders or double top/bottom are commonly found here.

Stage 4: End of trend

The last stage is when the trend begins to crumble and lose its staying power. In an uptrend, shortage of bullish newcomers halts the advance of higher prices, and some begin to take their profits, pushing the prices lower and lower. In a downtrend, a lack of new bears coming into the market stops the currency prices from going lower, and when they start to take profits, prices start going up. The crumbling and ending of a trend can come fast and furiously, without much warning to traders, or it can be a more prolonged process as power changes hands between the bulls and bears. Usually a trend reversal is brought about by a major change in the underlying sentiment about a currency. Jumping onto this stage of a trend in order to ride the underlying trend can be very risky as the trend is close to ending, and there is a high chance of the trade getting stopped out.

The most profitable entry points into a trend are at Stages 1 and 2, where the potential for the trend to grow and continue is great. Profit potential at Stage 3 may be limited as the trend has matured, and it is where most profit-taking takes place. When it comes to riding a trend, potential for loss becomes huge when getting in at Stage 4.

Using Currency Price Charts

One of the first steps to riding a trend requires the trader to identify the direction of the trend in the time frame that he or she is trading, and in another one or two bigger time frames as they will provide a wider perspective. Tagging along on the coattails of a trend is only fun if you are able to join in near the beginning or in the middle of it, not when the trend is starting to melt away. This ensures that you are able to capture the maximum profit possible from the trending movement of the currency pair, and not the meagre scraps or even possible losses found near the end of the trend.

Identifying the trend of a currency pair is achieved through the use of price charts. By using the information that you can gather from the chart alone, you can gain a better understanding of what is happening in the market.

For this strategy, I will show you how to make use of several technical tools that can help you identify which trend is in place, and to help maximise your trading profits. I shall start with the basic drawing tool of trendlines.

Trendlines

Trendline analysis is one of the most simple, yet effective, ways for forex traders to establish the direction of a trend, and to establish support and resistance levels on currency price charts. It is my number one favourite and fuss-free way of telling the trend direction of any currency pair. What a trendline does is to show you the price movements of the past, where people have bought or sold, and to give you an indication of where the market action could go next.

While some may dismiss or underestimate the power of trendline analysis as being retrospective and overly subjective in nature, trendlines can be very useful in helping you gauge the crowd in action, and which price levels were of concern to traders, and could be of concern in the future. Most important of all, it represents the underlying trend, and cuts out the noise of the market. Other than telling you the direction of the current trend, the trendlines also serve as areas where you could buy during an uptrend, or sell during a downtrend. It can even indicate points where you could buy and sell when prices oscillate in a trendline channel, where one trendline connects the highs of market action on one side, and another connects the lows on the other side.

A trendline is a dynamic line of support during an uptrend and a dynamic line of resistance during a downtrend. It slopes with the passing of time as buyers and sellers transact currencies at different prices. By using a trendline, you can tell which direction the currency prices are heading. If it is sloping upward, then the trend is up. If it is sloping downward, then a downtrend is in place.

As the market moves in a series of waves, with periods of expansion and contraction, tops and bottoms will form, and along these points, trendlines are drawn. Trendlines can be horizontal in a trading range, or ascending in an uptrend, or descending in a downtrend. (See Figure 6.2)

Figure 6.2: examples of trendlines

It is easy to find trendlines of any type on any time frame. On this 60-min chart of EUR/USD, you can see a downtrend defined by a down trendline, then a trading range marked by horizontal trendlines, followed by an uptrend defined by an up trendline. 'TLs' stand for trendlines on the chart.

Drawing trendlines

Trendlines do not just appear out of nowhere; you actually have to draw them into existence. For an up trendline, you draw a line connecting a series of lows, which get gradually higher. Your line need not necessarily connect all the bottoms of the uptrend, as long as it connects a minimum of two (preferably three) bottom points. This becomes your *up trendline*, with the trendline acting as support. (See Figure 6.3)

Figure 6.3: drawing an up trendline

The up trendline shown here connects a few bottom points to form a straight-edge line that slopes upward, forming a support line.

When drawing a down trendline, you draw a line connecting a series of highs, which get lower with time and, again, your line may not necessarily touch all the tops of the downtrend, as long as it connects a minimum of two (preferably three) rally points. This forms your *down trendline*, with the trendline acting as resistance.

You should track the low points of an uptrend, and the high points of a downtrend as these are areas where a predictable price response has taken place.

One thing about trendlines is that they tend to start from either an extreme low for an uptrend, or an extreme high for a downtrend and you can only determine these points in retrospect. While there is no doubt that applying trendlines to price charts can be quite subjective, it does not render them useless, in fact they are very practical technical tools.

To use high, low, or close?

When it comes to drawing trendlines, you may find yourself pondering whether to connect highs, lows or closing prices. Based on my own experience, I find it more useful to connect the highs or lows, rather than to construct trendlines using closing prices. Besides that, there are also other reasons to support why connecting highs or lows is better. Since the global currency market operates for 24 hours a day, for five and a half days a week, it can be quite inaccurate to track the opening and closing currency prices of the day as the day begins and ends at different times according to each time-zone.

For example, the Asian session opens and closes before the US market is open, so if you are to track the closing price, which closing price are you going to use? The Asian close or the US close? Some traders use GMT (Greenwich Mean Time), some American traders use EST (Eastern Standard Time), whereas others may prefer to use their local times on the price charts. Another reason why it is better to use high or low prices is due to the fact that these are extreme price points of a day, and these points are where there is the most resistance or support of the day, hence reflecting the market psychology better.

Measuring trend strength

As mentioned earlier, there are generally four stages of a trend: starting with the uncertainty of a new trend, then progressing into a fully charged trend, then slowing down its speed as it matures and, finally, the crumbling and ending of a trend. Adopting a high probability Trend Riding Strategy requires you to enter a trend at an appropriate timing, which will usually occur during a pull-back or a temporary pause in the trend before it resumes again. Preferably, you will want to join the trend somewhere between Stages 2 and 3, where there is still room for more price movement in the prevailing trend direction for your profit capture. Your entry into a trend must not be near its end as that will lower the probability of success of the trade.

Before you jump hastily onto a trend, it is best to first assess its strength at the given time. There are several ways of measuring the strength of a trend, and they are through the study of price action and through signals given by various indicators and oscillators.

Price action

There are some ways to gauge the strength of a trend according to the price chart:

1. trendline gradient;

2. correction or consolidation before the resumption of the main trend.

These are examined in more detail below.

1. Trendline gradient

One obvious tell-tale visual sign of the strength of a trend lies in the gradient of a trendline. A rule of thumb is that the steeper a trendline, the higher the chances of a trendline break, which will result in either a slower pace of price movement in the direction of the underlying trend or a trend reversal.

A steep trendline in an uptrend, for example, indicates the extreme enthusiasm of buyers as they bid up prices in a big magnitude move, and there are often no clear support levels on the charts. Such buying sprees tend to run out of steam quickly as all those who want to buy have already bought, and there is not enough influx of new buyers (see Figure 6.4). The reverse is true of a steep trendline in a downtrend, which indicates the extreme enthusiasm of sellers as they take every opportunity to sell.

Figure 6.4: example of steep trendline breaking

The steep up trendline on this daily chart of USD/CAD would not have been a good place to ride the uptrend as it would be difficult to sustain that enthusiastic level of buying interest for a long time. The lack of new USD/CAD bulls near the end of the trendline prevented the uptrend from continuing.

For the Trend Riding Strategy, it is best not to join in the trend when the trendline looks too steep as steep trendlines tend to give way to a less steep trendline or could end with a sharp reversal, and that may cause your trades to get stopped out unless you are willing to risk a lot for potentially very little, since the trend strength seems to be waning.

2. Correction or consolidation before the resumption of the main trend

The second way you can measure the strength of a trend is by examining the correction or consolidation period before the main trend continues. A trend cannot go on forever, without traders closing part or all of their positions for profit-taking. Hence, a trend is bound to experience a price pull-back of some sort even if it is in the midst of a strong uptrend or downtrend. A trend is assumed to be robust if corrections are short and consolidation periods are narrow.

Short corrections occur when prices do not retrace too much, and bounce off above a previous support in an uptrend or below a previous resistance level in a downtrend (see Figure 6.5). A short correction in an uptrend indicates that buyers of a currency pair have overwhelmed sellers or it could simply be that sellers are disinterested. In a downtrend, a short correction could indicate that bulls are no match for the aggressive bears. Whatever the reason is, this is a positive sign for the underlying trend.

Narrow consolidation periods are another strong continuation sign for the main trend. These consolidation periods may look like rectangles or flags (small rectangles) on currency price charts, and the magnitude of the corrective move is generally small (see Figure 6.5 again).

Figure 6.5: example of corrections

The downtrend seen on this daily chart of NZD/USD is an example of a strong trend, based on the observations that a corrective move bounced a good distance away from a previous resistance level, and that consolidation moves during the downtrend were quite small in magnitude.

In an uptrend, such narrow rectangles represent a slight battle between bulls and bears of a currency pair, buying pressure is typically sufficient to prevent a deeper correction of prices. Narrow rectangles in a downtrend, on the other hand, show that selling pressure at resistance is adequate in preventing prices from retracing too much. Although prices could break out of the rectangles in an opposite direction to the underlying trend, signalling a possible trend reversal in formation, the prevailing trend should be assumed to exist unless there is a sudden change in market sentiment or there are signs of trend reversal through technical indications.

When applying the Trend Riding Strategy, I suggest that you do not trade trends that seem likely to be in stage 4 as the probability of capturing profits can be quite low.

Technical signals

Before you evaluate the strength of a trend, you should already know the direction of the prevailing trend according to trendlines or moving averages. The main aim of evaluating the strength of a trend is to maximise your entry timing into an existing trend with the objective of a high-probability trade success. Other than looking at the currency price actions on the charts, you can make use of some technical tools to measure trend strength as well as to confirm the trend direction.

The Average Directional Index (ADX)

The Average Directional Index (ADX) is a popular indicator which many traders use to detect direction of trend and the trend strength. However, I find it to be extremely lagging and thus not so useful when it comes to applying it to price charts (See Figure 6.6).

The ADX is used to determine whether a market is trending, with values above 30 signifying a strong trend, and values below 20 indicating no trend or a trading range. As a measure of trend strength, the higher the ADX reading, the stronger the trend. This indicator does not distinguish between a bullish or bearish trend. As long as the reading is above 30, it means that either a strong uptrend or a strong downtrend could be in place.

Figure 6.6: Average Directional Index

This daily chart of USD/JPY illustrates that the strong uptrend that formed between July and October 2006 was not reflected at all on the ADX indicator (which lies in a separate window below the price chart) as the reading for this period was below 20, indicating the absence of a trend.

As I find the ADX to be extremely slow in reacting, and unable to indicate anything about the trend direction, I prefer to look at two other indicators, which are known as oscillators, to gauge trend strength as well as to confirm the trend direction.

Stochastic

The Stochastic is a very popular oscillator which was developed by George Lane in the late 1950s. The Stochastic is a momentum indicator that compares closing prices relative to high-low range over a specific time period. Stochastics are measured and represented by two different lines, %K and %D, and are plotted on a scale ranging from 0 to 100. Readings above 80 represent strong upward movement, while readings below 20 represent strong downward movements.

Once you have determined the direction of the trend using trendlines or moving averages, you should confirm it with the slope of the Slow Stochastic which indicates the momentum. In an uptrend, you should be looking for the Stochastic to slope strongly upward, whereas in a downtrend, the Stochastic should be sloping strongly downward, in accordance to the direction of the trend (see Figure 6.7).

In order to gauge the strength of a trend, when prices are making new highs or lows, the Stochastics should be making new highs or lows as well, and if it does so, you are relatively certain that the prevailing trend will continue. If the Stochastics are not doing the same, then that may signal a possible trend reversal.

Figure 6.7: Stochastic

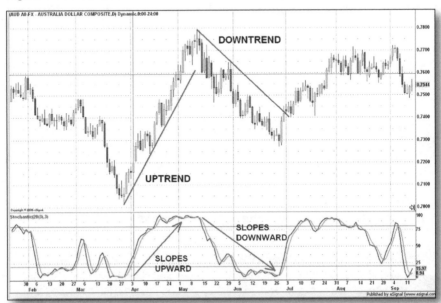

As AUD/USD rallied in an uptrend, Slow Stochastic sloped upward accordingly, and as AUD/USD declined in a downtrend, Slow Stochastic sloped downward accordingly as well.

The Moving Average Convergence/Divergence (MACD) histogram

An alternative to using the Stochastics is the moving average convergence/divergence (MACD) histogram. The MACD histogram is useful for anticipating changes in trend. Similarly, you should be looking for MACD histogram to slope upward during an uptrend, and for it to slope downward during a downtrend. When prices are moving higher or moving lower, the histogram should become bigger as the speed of the price movement accelerates, and the histogram should contract as price movement decelerates. That is, if a currency pair is rallying with strength, the histogram should be positive and growing larger (see Figure 6.8). If a currency pair is declining strongly, the histogram should be negative and growing larger. That is how traders can make use of MACD histogram to gauge the strength of a price move.

Figure 6.8: MACD

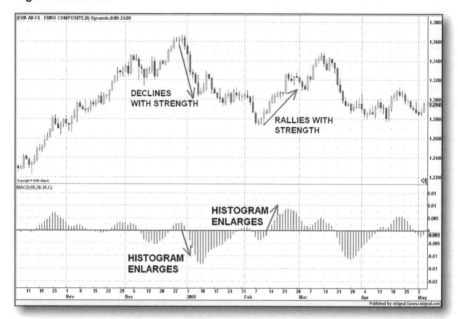

The initial phase of EUR/USD decline caused the MACD histogram to enlarge in size, illustrating that the speed of decline was fast and furious. But in the later phase of downtrend, the histogram became smaller, reflecting the slow speed of price decline. The histogram enlarged again when EUR/USD rallied with gusto, but when the bullish momentum slowed down, the histogram decreased in size too.

Now that you have become acquainted with the tools of identifying the trend direction and measuring of trend strength, I will show you some of the basic effective steps to riding the trend.

Technical Execution Of The Strategy

To ride a trend successfully, you should get confirmation from the price action or technical signals that a trend is in place, and should avoid getting into trends which are already near the ending stage. There is no need for you to predict what the market is going to do, because you can never know that for sure, but the next best thing is perhaps to just go along with what the market *is* doing, and trend riding allows you to achieve that.

Trading a trendline bounce can be a very profitable, yet simple, strategy for joining an existing trend as it provides a relatively low-risk entry point for traders. Here are the steps of this strategy:

1. First determine how long you wish to ride the trend for because that will influence the time frame of the trend you will ride on.

2. Make sure that the current market sentiment agrees with the technicals. If not,

3. Note the gradient of the trendline in both time frames and the number of times it has been tested.

4. Confirm trend direction and trend strength with oscillators.

5. Enter a limit entry or market entry order based on the hourly or daily trendline, depending on your preferred time horizon.

6. Place stop-loss orders at least 20 pips on the other side of the trendline.

I will now go through these steps with you with a more detailed explanation of what to look out for when adopting this strategy.

1. Determine your holding period

Since many people like to day trade the forex market, I will highlight two suitable time frames for this trading horizon: the daily and hourly time frames. Even if you trade intraday, it is necessary for you to use at least the hourly chart to plan your trade even though you may be using the 5-minute or 15-minute chart to monitor your trade. In my opinion, it is essential for day traders to know the trend direction on the daily chart as this enables them to trade knowing the overall technical picture.

2. Make sure that the current market sentiment agrees with the technicals

The forex market is mainly driven by the players' perceptions of fundamental news, and technicals usually follow the market sentiment. Hence, you should look for the market sentiment to be supportive of the trade, in the direction of the prevailing trend. If the market sentiment appears to be shifting, and the prevailing trend seems to be threatened, you should give the trendline bounce a miss. However, if the sentiment agrees, you can proceed with the rest of the strategy as outlined.

3. Note the gradient of the trendline on both time frames and the number of times it has been tested

As mentioned earlier, for the Trend Riding Strategy I prefer to stay out of joining a trend that is on a very steep trendline (See Figure 6.9), but that really is up to you, depending on your own risk appetite and trading style.

Figure 6.9: avoid trends with steep gradients

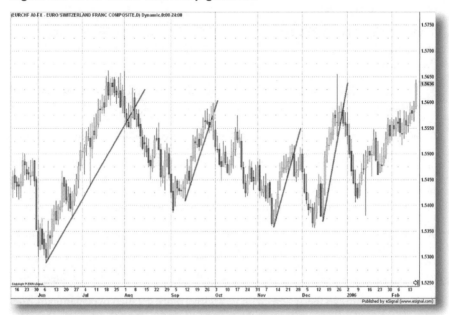

The up trendlines drawn on this daily chart of EUR/CHF were not suitable for trading trendline bounces due to their steep gradient.

4. Confirm trend direction and trend strength with oscillators

Ideally, either Stochastics or MACD histogram should be sloping upward when trading an upside bounce (off an up trendline), or sloping downward when trading a downside bounce (off a down trendline). However, this condition is not a prerequisite as these oscillators may lag if the momentum is not accelerating, but if you can get additional confirmation from the oscillators then the probability of success will be higher.

5. Enter a limit entry or market entry order on the hourly or daily trendline, depending on your preferred time horizon

The problem with placing a limit entry order is that sometimes the price may not reach your limit to open your position, and you could end up with an "either my price or none" situation, missing out on the opportunity to trade a trendline bounce. One way of securing your place on the trend bounce is to initiate your trade a few pips before the price-trendline touch (see the following chart).

Figure 6.10: trendline bounce

The letters A and C on this 60-min chart of EUR/JPY indicate where the price did not touch the trendline exactly, while B indicates where the price had moved slightly beyond the trendline. All these three instances are examples of successful trendline bounces.

6. Place stop-loss orders at least 20 pips on the other side of the trendline

Having tight stops is the worst enemy of this strategy. It is very common for currency prices to exceed and pierce the trendline, even a daily one, by 10-15 pips or more in a very fast-paced move, and then just as quickly retreat back into the main price territory on the action side of the trendline. This move is often orchestrated by institutional players to hit the accumulation of stops beyond the trendline so as to sweep money off weak hands into their own pockets. Of course, sometimes the prices may pierce 20 plus pips through the trendline, and then make a U-turn back into the old territory, resuming the underlying trend.

Note: There is no one-size-fits-all stop loss level that is the "best", as that will depend on how long you intend to hold your position for and your lot size.

Summary

The idea of riding a trend is age-old, and there is nothing sexy about it. However, timing your entry into an existing trend can be the trickiest part of this strategy. One effective way of riding the trend is to sneak in during a trend pull-back, which you can do by trading trendline bounces, in the direction of the underlying trend. The nature of the forex market makes trading bounces during an uptrend or downtrend a breeze as there are no uptick rules or restrictions on shorting a currency pair. Always keep in mind that when you trade, the direction should be in line with the current market sentiment, and if not, it is better to pass up the bounce.

7:
Strategy 3 –
Breakout Fading

Strategy 3 – Breakout Fading

Support and resistance levels, whether they are found amidst chart patterns, indicators or along trendlines, are an indication of where a predictable price response can be expected. A support level is where buying pressure overwhelms selling pressure enough to interrupt or reverse a downtrend. A sturdy support level is more likely to hold up even if prices slightly pierce through the support, and that presents traders with an excellent buying opportunity.

Conversely, a resistance level is where selling pressure is strong enough to overcome buying pressure such that an uptrend can be stopped temporarily or reversed. A strong resistance level is more likely to block further advance even if prices slightly pierce through the resistance, and such a situation presents traders with an excellent shorting opportunity.

You can take advantage of such opportunities by *fading breakouts*.

Fading breakouts refers to trading against breakouts, when you believe that the currency prices will not be able to sustain a follow-through action in the direction of the breakout. We fade breakouts when we expect breakouts from support and resistance levels to be false and unsustainable, especially when those support and resistance levels are of great significance. Many breakouts tend to fail at the first few attempts, and that makes fading breakouts an excellent short-term strategy for forex traders. Fading breakouts tends to be more effective as a short-term strategy, and is not meant for the long-term. False breakouts, also known as *fakeouts*, are a bane for breakout traders, but boon for breakout faders.

The Crowd Likes to Trade Breakouts

The idea of trading breakouts appeals to many independent traders, especially newcomers to the currency market. Support and resistance levels are seen as price floor and price ceiling respectively. A support level attracts buyers' enthusiasm for higher bids, and prevents the price from going lower, while a resistance level attracts sellers' enthusiasm for shorting, and prevents the price from advancing higher. Thus, it is perfectly logical for the crowd to think that if the support level is penetrated, then the general price move should be downward, and hence they are more likely to sell than to buy. The opposite is true for a price break above a resistance level. When that happens, the crowd will usually come to the conclusion that if the resistance level is penetrated, then prices are more likely to advance higher in a rally, and hence they are more likely to buy than to sell.

Knowing this, it is very easy to see why there tends to be a big cluster of entry stop orders placed just above a resistance level and also placed just below a support level.

However, the cluster of stop orders there does not just comprise entry orders, but also stop-loss orders placed by traders who have bought near the support level, or have sold near the resistance level. So if the currency price crosses above the resistance level, short positions will be stopped out. In an opposite fashion, long positions will be stopped out when the currency price crosses below the support level.

Why Most Breakouts Fail

One of the most compelling reasons why most breakouts tend to fail is due to the fact that winners need to take money from losers, and it does not always pay to have the same mentality as the crowd, as the majority will crash out of the trading game broke. Money has to be made from the majority, not from the minority who get it right. The crowd holds the dumb money with weak hands, whereas the smart money tends to belong to the domain of big players who can afford to reach into their deep pockets for a couple of tricks to sabotage the crowd. The most money is made when the crowd turns out to be wrong, because then these players will scramble to get out of their losing positions, causing vertical rallies or declines.

If almost everyone, ranging from people hanging out in online forums to your neighbours, see the same great opportunity to buy above a resistance level or sell below a support level, who will be the sellers on the other side of the transaction?

For someone to buy something, there must be a seller, and vice versa. Granted, there are not too many traders who are indeed unaware of such a level, so how can the majority make money from the minority? If there is so much market demand to buy above a resistance or sell below a support, the market maker has to absorb all those one-sided orders and take the other side of the equation. However, we must be aware that the market maker is certainly no fool.

Trading against the crowd

I have increasingly noticed that obvious support and resistance levels on the currency price charts tend to provide the best opportunities for fading breakouts, although it is not always the case. This is not surprising, given the fact that the most well-recognised price levels or chart patterns will be detected by the majority of traders. Almost everyone is taught the same aspects of technical analysis from books or other sources, and new traders are the ones who tend to most eagerly follow trade recommendations stemming from the formation of certain chart patterns on the currency price charts.

Retail traders like to trade breakouts, but institutional, or the more seasoned traders, prefer to fade breakouts, doing exactly the opposite of what the majority is expected to do. That is one of the main reasons why most breakouts fail – the institutional or seasoned traders taking advantage of the crowd psychology of the retail or inexperienced traders, and winning at their expense. Our strategy is to trade in the direction of institutional activity, by fading breakouts.

Tricks of Institutional Dealers and Traders

Before I talk about the Breakout Fading Strategy, let's understand a bit more about the kind of tricks that are played by institutional dealers and traders.

Many market makers, banks, and hedge funds – mainly big players with deep pockets – are known to fade breakouts, which are traded by many retail traders. Their game plan is to make money from the majority of the crowd who thinks that the price will rally merrily after an upside breakout or decline dangerously after a downside breakout. Since market makers are the pricing counterparties to their retail customers, they have to take the opposite end of your trade, whether you like it or not.

First of all, let's see things from their point of view. For example, if there is an expected crowd demand to buy at a certain price above a resistance level, these firms know that they will have to sell to their customers, so how will they position themselves in an advantageous position? What they routinely do is that they reach into their pockets, spend a bit of money buying up the currency pair to the level where stop entry (and stop-loss) orders have been placed by their customers, so that they can now sell to those people who are desperate to buy, thus making some decent profits from this trick.

The next stage of this trick comes when customers' stop (both entry and exit) orders are triggered and the retail crowd goes long. This gives the market makers and other big players a chance to close the previous longs they entered by selling to the crowd. However, the big players know they can make money in both directions, so now they begin shorting to overwhelm the buying pressure from the crowd, thus pushing the currency prices down, back below the breakout level, where many stop-loss orders have been placed by the buyers who trade the upside breakout. These stop-loss orders then become executed, and the big players can gleefully offload all or some of their shorts by buying from those who are selling to close their losing breakout trades (See Figure 7.1).

Figure 7.1: market makers and breakouts

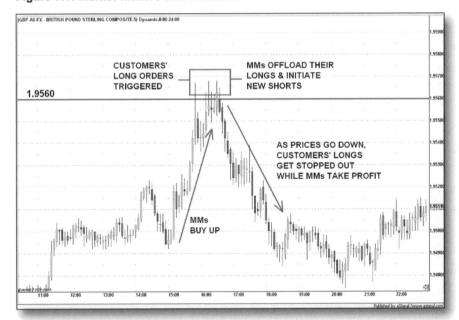

This 5-min chart of GBP/USD on 11 December 2006 shows how market makers (denoted as "MMs") pushed the currency pair up above the resistance level (1.9560) to trigger stops, and after taking their profits, they then pushed prices back down for further gains.

This is the story behind the false breakout – beautiful in the eyes of big institutional players; hideous and greatly undesirable in the eyes of the crowd. Hedge funds, with their immense capital, can play these tricks on the unsuspecting crowd as well, even though they trade only for themselves.

Market makers have the information of where their customers' orders are from their order book. Even if these big players have good intentions, they could still potentially trade against you so as to cover imbalanced trades or to supply liquidity to the market. Of course, trading to maximise profits of their internal accounts cannot be ruled out. A potential conflict of interest can thus exist, and retail traders must know that in order to know how to protect themselves. After all, market makers exist to give profit to their share-holders, not to their customers.

When big players go on a stop hunting spree, false breakouts are likely to be the consequence of that. The crowd may think that the false breakout is due to the sudden turning of the market, but it is most likely the direct result of the games that big players play. Taking out stops placed by the crowd at predictable levels serve their monetary interests. Retail traders must know what these big players are doing or are thinking of doing in order to join in their game of scooping up money from the majority of the crowd.

False breakouts also arise when market makers execute stops before the interbank market has reached those prices or execute stops that lie just outside the actual trading area. Sometimes you may see that prices have pierced slightly through the breakout level in intraday charts, or even longer-term charts like the daily charts, and then make a quick U-turn back into the pre-breakout price zone.

Lack of fresh blood

False breakouts do not just happen because of the tricks institutional players use; they could also be the result of the market running out of steam to reach higher highs or lower lows in a sustained price break. This situation occurs when there are not enough fresh buyers to sustain an upward price move or fresh sellers to sustain a downward price move. The lack of new blood into an already very long or short market often heralds an unexpected turn of the market as the market move becomes attenuated.

Identifying The Opportunities

Since big players like to fade breakouts, individual traders have a higher chance of success if they fade breakouts as well. Fading breakouts is not an instinctive thing to do as a trader, because the prospect of reaping massive gains from a price breakout outweighs the prospect of a failed breakout, and of course, everyone is greedy for big easy profits. Even though fading breakouts is counter-intuitive, it can be a very profitable strategy for capturing short-term gains. In order to maximise the effectiveness of this strategy, you need to go through some analysis steps which will guide you as to where and when you can fade a price breakout with a higher probability of success. The key points to look out for are the location and the timing.

Where potential fakeouts occur

You can use false breakouts to your advantage instead of seeing them as your enemies. The first question to ask is: where do false breakouts usually occur? False breakouts can be found anywhere on the currency price chart at levels of support and resistance, which may manifest in the form of trendlines, chart patterns or previous daily highs or lows. I recommend that you look for opportunities on a minimum time frame of hourly or more. There are really no hard and fast rules regarding the entry criteria, as there is absolutely no way of predicting with 100% accuracy the next price movement.

Trendlines

There are similarities between riding a trend through trading trendline bounces which I have covered in Chapter 6, and trading false breakouts of trendlines. In both cases, we are expecting the price to bounce off the trendline, whether the price has or has not touched, or has pierced slightly through the trendline.

I have observed that the probability of a false breakout is higher if the trendline has a gentle gradient of slope, especially if it is angled at 45° or less. You don't have to gauge that with a protractor; just a visual analysis will do.

Such a gently sloping trendline can usually be drawn by connecting at least two extreme points of highs or lows over a long period of time, depending on whether it is a downtrend or an uptrend. There should ideally be some decent amount of open space between these two or three extreme points of contact, indicating that prices have deviated away from the trendline in the direction of the current trend (See Figure 7.2).

Usually, the third or even fourth extreme point of contact on the gently sloping trendline presents a good fading opportunity, especially if a moving average lies slightly below the ascending trendline or slightly above the descending trendline.

The speed of price movement preceding the approach to the trendline must also be considered. If prices are approaching slowly and steadily towards the trendline, then a false breakout or a trendline bounce would most likely occur.

On the other hand, a fast and high amplitude move could very likely result in a successful price breakout of the trendline with a sustained follow-through in prices, aided by the boost of momentum. In that case, it is better to refrain from fading the breakout (See Figure 7.3).

Figure 7.2: fading opportunities

A gently sloping down trendline is drawn on a 60-min chart of USD/CHF. Note that the gradient of the trendline is angled around 45°, and there is some amount of space between the extreme points of contact, which makes it a good opportunity to fade a potential breakout at the third and fourth extreme point of contact.

Figure 7.3: fading opportunity to avoid

Although the up trendline on this 60-min chart of USD/CHF is angled at less than 45°, it does not make a good candidate for fading breakouts due to the currency pair having just declined by about 60 pips in the hour preceding the breakout attempt (a fast and high amplitude move). The pair was able to break out successfully from the up trendline following the very bearish momentum.

Technical execution

Place a limit or market entry order a few pips below a down trendline or above an up trendline in order to catch the potential bounce. If you are a more aggressive type of trader, you may choose to stagger your entry by placing another order a few pips after the breakout. This is a form of dollar-cost averaging whereby the average cost of entry becomes more favourable for either your long position (fading a downside breakout) or short position (fading an upside breakout). Staggering your entry points can help to optimise your overall cost of entry, and it must be done according to a proper money management plan. Stops should be placed at least 20-30 pips beyond the support or resistance, outside of the price zone.

Chart patterns

The amazing power of technical analysis has been discovered by more and more traders, especially those who are involved in trading forex. Nowadays, with the majority of forex traders utilising some form of technical analysis in their decision-making process, chart patterns have become easily recognisable by experienced traders, although not as easily and quickly by inexperienced traders.

In order to employ the Breakout Fading Strategy, you have to know where to look for these false breakouts to occur. Having just discussed trendline fakeouts, let me go through with you some common technical formations where false breakouts are likely to occur in currency price charts. Keep in mind that consistent outcomes cannot be expected of chart pattern formations, and that the Breakout Fading Strategy must be applied with a lot of common sense, like with all other trading strategies.

Head-and-Shoulders

This chart pattern is one of the hardest for new traders to recognise at first, and can take a while to pick up the visual recognition. Nonetheless, it is one of the most widely taught chart patterns in technical analysis.

The head-and-shoulders pattern consists of three points of rallies, with the second rally (the head) being the highest, flanked by a smaller rally on the left and right side (the shoulders). The pattern resembles the head and shoulders outline of a human being, and is thus named. A horizontal or sloping trendline, known as the neckline, can be drawn connecting the lows of the left and right shoulders linking to the head (See Figure 7.4).

Figure 7.4: head-and-shoulders pattern

A head-and-shoulders pattern is spotted on a daily chart of AUD/USD. The pattern consists of the head, which is the final rally of the pattern, separated by two smaller rallies, known as shoulders, which need not be identical in height (amplitude of price move) or width (duration of time).

The head-and-shoulders pattern is usually found at the end or middle of an uptrend. A similar, but inverted head-and-shoulders pattern can also be found at the end or middle of a downtrend. This inverse head-and-shoulders pattern consists of three points of declines, with the second decline (the head) having the lowest low, separated by two smaller declines (the left and right shoulders).

Head-and-shoulders can occur as reversal or continuation formations. If the pattern is found at the end of an uptrend, it could signal a bearish reversal or consolidation period before the uptrend is continued. If it is found at the end of a downtrend, it could signal a bullish reversal or consolidation period before resuming the downtrend. Head-and-shoulders reversal patterns are notorious for precipitating false breakouts, and hence are good places to fade a breakout.

Why are false breakouts so common with this pattern?

Many traders who have identified this formation have their stop-loss orders below the neckline if they are buying up the rallies from the support level. The reverse is true for traders placing stop-loss orders above the neckline of an inverse head-and-shoulders pattern if they are shorting the decline from the resistance level. Besides stop-loss orders, there can also be numerous entry stop orders placed below the neckline or above the inverse neckline in anticipation of a price breakout, leading the way to a trend reversal.

When the head-and-shoulders pattern experiences a false breakout, prices will usually rebound, and may stage an explosive price movement off the neckline in the pre-breakout zone. This is because traders who have shorted the downside breakout or who have longed the upside breakout will have their stops triggered when currencies move in the opposite direction against their positions. Most of the time, these fakeouts are triggered by big players who want to shake out positions of small players.

Technical execution

It is best to assume that the first break of a head-and-shoulders pattern tends to be false. Based on this assumption, you may fade the breakout with a limit or market entry order a few pips above the neckline or below the inverse neckline, and may even choose to stagger your entry by placing another order a few pips beyond the neckline when the price breaks through it. The stop should be placed at least 20-30 pips beyond the neckline outside of the price zone (See Figure 7.5).

As for profit objective, it depends on the time frame of holding your positions open. Technically, you may choose to place it slightly below the high of the second shoulder, or slightly above the low of the second shoulder of the inverse head and shoulder formation. If the current market sentiment supports the case for a very strong rebound or trend continuation, you may wish to set a higher objective by taking profits nearer the head, and hold it for several days or weeks for the objective to be reached, depending on your own preference.

Figure 7.5: fading breakout from a head-and-shoulders pattern

A head-and-shoulders pattern on a daily chart of NZD/JPY provided a very good opportunity to fade a potential breakout from the neckline. According to the strategy, you can place a limit or market buy order a few pips above the neckline, and a stop 20-30 pips below the neckline. Profit limit orders can be placed near the high of the second shoulder or near the top of the head. In this case, both profit targets would have been achieved.

Double top and double bottom

Double tops and double bottoms are easily recognisable by most traders on currency price charts, and their appearance signals a potential trend reversal.

A double top formation consists of two rally peaks separated by a valley. The two peaks need not be of the same height for the pattern to be considered a double top. When the price breaks below the neckline connecting the valley low and the base of the peaks, it signals a possible downside breakout (See Figure 7.6). Hence, many traders place their entry stop orders below the neckline of a double top in anticipation for a trend reversal to the downside.

Figure 7.6: double top

EUR/USD broke out successfully to the downside from the neckline of a double top formation present in this daily chart.

A double bottom is simply an inverted image of a double top, and works the opposite way. It is made up of two bottom lows separated by a rally, and when the price penetrates above the neckline joining the rally high and the base of the bottoms, it signals a possible upside breakout (See Figure 7.7). As you would expect, many traders place their entry stop orders above the neckline of a double bottom in anticipation for a trend reversal to the upside.

Figure 7.7: double bottom

EUR/USD broke out successfully to the upside from the neckline of a double bottom formation present in this daily chart.

These chart formations face the same problem of being easily recognised by traders in that every one does the same thing of placing orders at the same predictable price level, making easy bait for institutional players to sweep money off the table again. Recall that our strategy is to trade in the direction of institutional activity, and we do this by fading the first attempt of a price breakout.

Technical execution

Even if the price does not exceed the neckline of the double top or bottom, a position may be opened with a limit or market entry order a few pips above the neckline of a double top or a few pips below the neckline of a double bottom in order to catch the bounce. As with fading breakouts of other chart patterns, you can even choose to stagger your entry by placing another order a few pips beyond the neckline when the price breaks through it (See Figure 7.8).

Figure 7.8: fading breakout from a double bottom

This daily chart of USD/CAD shows a double bottom formation. According to the strategy, you can place entry orders a few pips below the neckline or above the neckline in order to fade the breakout. USD/CAD indeed broke above the neckline by 22 pips in a false breakout move before going downhill over the next few weeks.

The stop should be placed at least 20-30 pips beyond the neckline outside of the price zone. The profit objective may be set slightly below the previous peak of a double top or slightly above the previous low of a double bottom. The rationale for placing your profit target there is that there is a strong chance that prices may rebound from the previous peak or bottom level, and form a triple top or bottom, even though such formations are less common than double tops or bottoms. Triple tops or bottoms represent a more extended fight between bulls and bears of a currency pair.

Best market condition to fade breakouts

One persistent trading conundrum is for a trader to decide when is the best time to trade a breakout and when to trade against it. I know traders who only fade breakouts, and also people from the camp that only trade breakouts. In the forex trading business, good traders cannot afford to be rigid in their mindset and follow preconceived rules without much thoughts and analysis. The guidelines that I have laid out for fading breakouts, should be just that – guidelines, not definite rules carved in stone. Even though the general rule of thumb is to fade breakouts on the first attempt, you need to take into consideration the various circumstances that present optimal or less than ideal fading opportunities.

Adopt the Breakout Fading Strategy only when you sense a high probability of the market situation supporting it. Not only must you spot a good location to carry out this strategy, perfect timing is also a key ingredient to spotting an ideal fading opportunity. From my experience, the best market condition for fading breakouts is a range-bound market.

Range-bound markets

It is common knowledge that financial markets spend most of their time bouncing back and forth between a range of prices trapped between a support and resistance level, instead of always making fresh higher highs or lower lows in an uptrend or downtrend. The forex market is no exception, and tends to stay range-bound most of the time, in between trending phases.

Fading breakouts can be a very profitable trading strategy when the market is ranging. A range is bound by a support level and a resistance level which are in close proximity to each other, as buyers and sellers of a currency pair battle it out after either side has established an extreme overbought or oversold price zone. This period of consolidation settles the currency prices within a range, and may be manifested in the form of a rectangle (a horizontal channel) or a triangle, whereby neither bulls nor bears of a currency pair are stronger than the other. At some point, either the bulls or the bears will wrestle control and overpower the other party, marking the start of a trending phase again.

A trading range should consist of at least two contact points at the support and at the resistance levels drawn. It is preferable to fade breakouts at the third or even fourth contact points at these levels on the hourly or daily charts as they tend to be more reliable (See Figure 7.9). Fading breakouts in a rectangle or triangle involves buying at the support line and selling at the resistance line at the third or fourth contact point on either side, unless there are overwhelming signs that the market is ready to trend again.

Figure 7.9: range-bound market

> A trading range in the form of a horizontal channel or a rectangle is seen on this 60-min chart of EUR/CHF. This rectangle provided excellent fading opportunities whereby you can sell at the resistance and buy at the support at the third, fourth and even fifth contact points.

The Breakout Fading Strategy tends not to work as well for strong trending phases of the market, and is more effective in range-bound market conditions. That said, you can still fade a breakout while in a strong trend, if you can contend with a very small profit objective of not more than 20-30 pips. So whether or not you fade a breakout during a trending phase really depends on your own preference, degree of risk appetite and experience in the market.

Summary

There are times when it is better to follow the crowd, and there are times when we should deviate from it. The Breakout Fading Strategy requires the trader to think of what the crowd would do in the given situation based on the chart or price patterns and market conditions, and then act the opposite way of what the crowd would do.

For the independent trader to have success on his or her side, he or she must think like the big institutional players, and stick to what these players are likely to do.

From my experience trading the forex market, I think it is better to be skeptical of any first breakout attempt from a significant level. While not every breakout fading trade will turn out profitable, knowing how to identify high probability entries can improve your odds of success when trading this strategy.

8:
Strategy 4 –
Breakout Trading

Strategy 4 – Breakout Trading

Who hasn't harboured the thought of reaping massive profits from a big price move in a short time?

Despite the notoriety associated with trading breakouts, it remains one of the most basic concepts in trading. A breakout typically occurs when the currency price moves beyond a period of consolidation or trading range, or when the price penetrates above or below an established price level, which can be a resistance or support level, resulting in a follow-through of prices past those levels, whether temporarily or permanently. The price movement past a breakout point can either be a short or a more sustained affair, and that may depend on the time frame of prices that you are looking at.

Even though big market players tend to fade breakouts, and it is better for retail traders to side with these players, it does not mean that trading breakouts is entirely a bad idea. Breakout trading does have merits, and a different set of rules as compared to fading breakouts.

As mentioned in Chapter 7 on breakout fading, it is better to first assume that any breakout from a significant level is false, as false breakouts are more common than successful breakouts. However, there are times when trading breakouts can be very profitable, even though breakouts are known to be technically unstable. Hence, in order to trade breakouts with a higher probability of success, you have to incorporate as many market factors as possible, including both technical and fundamental analysis, to get a better feel of the current overall market sentiment.

The problem of lack of volume data

While volume is critical to the trading of breakout in other asset classes like stocks or futures, in the forex market traders lack the knowledge of volume since there is no central exchange to monitor all the transactions that have gone through or are going through. Lack of forex volume data is a huge disadvantage to forex traders as volume often reveals where the market is positioned or is positioning, and is often an important criteria of any breakout trading strategies as successful breakouts are generally accompanied by a rise in volume. In view of that, you have to rely on several guidelines so that you can position yourself for a potentially good breakout.

Types of Breakouts

When a price attempts a breakout of a significant support or resistance level, it signals a change in the balance of supply and demand, and such a change may be triggered by a change in market sentiment, or a renewed resolution of bulls or bears of a currency pair, or the unfolding of certain fundamental events. Successful breakouts must be accompanied with a strong surge of momentum in the direction of the price breakout.

Price breakouts can be categorised into two main types:

1. continuation breakouts, and

2. reversal breakouts.

According to the basic tenet of technical analysis, one should always assume the underlying trend to continue unless proved otherwise, and it is no exception in this case.

Continuation breakout

In a continuation breakout, currency prices break out of established price levels to resume the underlying trend, by climbing higher in a continuation of an uptrend, or by falling lower in a downtrend. Usually, a breakout occurs after a period of consolidation in which when buyers and sellers of a currency pair regroup and contemplate the next price move (See Figure 8.1).

Figure 8.1: continuation breakout

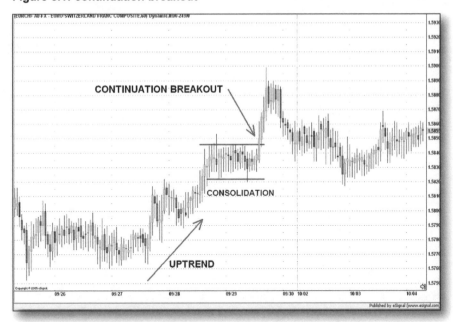

A continuation breakout is seen on this 60-min chart of EUR/CHF as prices broke out from a short period of consolidation to resume the uptrend.

Reversal breakout

Sometimes, a current trend may be near its last stage, and could be in the process of reversing as the hype fuelling the trend is extinguished. In such a situation, a breakout could lead to a trend reversal and the beginning of a new trend, hence it being a reversal breakout (See Figure 8.2).

Figure 8.2: reversal breakout

A reversal breakout is seen on this 60-min chart of GBP/JPY as prices broke out from a period of consolidation to reverse the trend from a prior uptrend to a downtrend.

False breakouts

However, there are many times when prices do not move in a straightforward direction (whether continuation or reversal) in the real trading world. Traders observing a price breakout could be treated to a display of the infamous false breakout which all breakout traders fear and detest. A false breakout occurs when the price has pierced through the support or resistance level, but then retreats back into the previous price zone, thus stopping out most breakout traders if their stops are just below the support or above the resistance level. Institutional players are often the culprits behind false breakouts as they manipulate the currency price past common stop levels so as to deliberately clean out that side of the market.

The worst kind of breakout is the whipsaw type, whereby prices move out of the price range, then back into the range, and then break out of the level again, stopping both breakout traders and faders at least once (See Figure 8.3). A whipsaw breakout usually occurs when there is lack of momentum behind the price move or when the breakout is small and weak. What makes a breakout unsustainable is the lack of subsequent waves of buyers or sellers of a currency pair to generate more buying or selling interest in an upside or downside breakout respectively after the first wave of buyers or sellers has jumped in shortly after the breakout. Sometimes, the price action can be so choppy that it is better to stay out of the market.

Figure 8.3: whipsaw-type breakout

A whipsaw-type breakout is seen on this 60-min chart of GBP/USD as prices first broke out by 30 pips from the resistance level, then went back into the pre-breakout zone, and then broke out of the resistance level again. Such whipsaw action tends to stop out both breakout traders and faders in the process.

With so many different outcomes of a breakout, all breakouts must be treated with some degree of suspicion, even if you have iron-clad reasons not to doubt the direction of your trade, they all carry some risk of failure. That is when reasonably placed stops can help preserve the rest of your capital when a price breakout does not go your way.

Measuring Reversal Breakouts

Trading a reversal breakout undoubtedly sounds very appetising to many traders who are lured to it by the prospect of attaining easy big profits in little time. Who doesn't like to get a reserved seat at the turnaround of a trend as the ride gets propelled by a frenzied momentum? However, things are certainly not as simple as they may seem on the surface.

First of all, how do you know if a breakout is going to reverse the current trend?

To get some clues as to whether a trend could be reversing, you should scrutinise the currency price charts, and look out for certain reversal chart patterns that tend to serve as harbingers of a trend change. Examples of such patterns include the head-and-shoulders, double top/bottom, triple top/bottom and so on. If you do spot these formations in your charts especially in the daily or weekly chart, there is a high chance that a reversal may be in the works, and that you should get ready for trading a breakout.

In addition to these chart patterns, you can also make use of momentum indicators to tell you if a trend is nearing its end.

Using momentum indicators

Momentum indicators, also known as oscillators, often lead price actions, and they help to alert traders to turning points such as a trend reversal breakout.

Moving Average Convergence/Divergence (MACD)

MACD is one of the simplest yet most dependable indicators available in the toolbox of a trader. MACD consists of three exponential moving averages, even though only two lines appear on the chart. The MACD line itself is the difference between a currency pair's 12-period and 26-period exponential moving averages (EMA). Usually, a signal line made up of a 9-period EMA of the MACD line is plotted together with MACD. A bullish signal is given when the MACD line crosses above its signal line, and a bearish signal occurs when the MACD line crosses below its signal line.

A better visual representation of MACD was invented by Thomas Aspray in the form of a MACD histogram, which is made up of a series of vertical lines. The histogram simply represents the difference between the MACD line and its signal line, and is plotted around the zero line. The histogram is positive (above zero line) when the MACD line is above its signal line, and is negative (below zero line) when the MACD line is below its signal line (See Figure 8.4).

Figure 8.4: MACD

> Note the MACD indicator in the lower section of the chart window, directly below the price chart section. You can see that the histogram rises above the zero line when MACD line lies above the signal line, and goes below the zero line when MACD line moves below the signal line.

The MACD histogram tracks the speed of the price movement, and reflects the speed by the way it slopes. For example, if a price move accelerates with an upside breakout to a level higher as buyers are in a frenzy to buy the currency, then other buyers will be eager to join in as they anticipate a continuation of the rally at the same time that many people who have shorted are being stopped out, pushing the rally higher. Under such circumstances, the histogram should become bigger (each line becoming longer than the previous line) as the speed of the price movement accelerates in a quick rally. On the other hand, when the price movement decelerates, the histogram should contract (each line becoming shorter than the previous line) accordingly. The reverse is true for a downside breakout.

MACD divergence signals

If you want to detect a trend reversal breakout, there is a way you can exploit this momentum feature of MACD, and that is through MACD divergence signals.

When a currency pair rallies to a new high, or moves sideways, but the MACD histogram declines, then a bearish divergence is formed (see Figure 8.5). The bearish divergence in MACD mostly takes place above the zero line because prior upward price movement would have resulted in MACD moving into positive territory. A bullish divergence in MACD results when a currency pair declines to a new low or moves sideways, but the MACD histogram slopes up higher instead of sloping lower.

Figure 8.5: MACD divergence signal

Although USD/CHF made new highs on the daily chart, the MACD histogram did not and, instead, declined lower, shrinking the histogram in the process. This bearish divergence signalled that momentum was decreasing despite USD/CHF making new highs, and gave a strong clue that a price reversal could be in place. In the following few days after the new high in USD/CHF, the pair declined by about 400 pips.

Hence, when you spot a potential breakout scenario on a currency price chart, you should also take note of how the MACD histogram is performing. If the currency has been making new highs, has the MACD histogram been doing the same by forming higher peaks? If so, you can assume that the uptrend is still in place, and perhaps any breakout to the downside would be short-lived or probably false. However, if the MACD histogram shows a bearish divergence, then you will have a strong signal that a downside breakout is more likely to be sustained than false. The reverse applies to a bullish divergence. Although an MACD divergence signal seldom occurs, it is generally a very strong reliable signal when it does make an appearance.

Relative Strength Index (RSI)

Another momentum indicator that can help you anticipate rather than react to price changes especially when prices are at the verge of breaking out is the RSI. The RSI measures the relative changes between higher and lower closing prices over a given time period, and provides an indication of overbought and oversold conditions.

This is the formula for RSI:

```
RSI = 100 - 100 / (1 + RS)

where
RS  = (total gains / n) / (total losses / n)
n   = number of RSI periods
```

A reading of 30 or below indicates that the currency pair is in an oversold condition, and a reading of 70 or above indicates that the currency pair is in an overbought condition. However, it is not so useful to use this overbought/oversold condition for gauging the outlook of a potential breakout on the currency price chart as momentum indicators do not work as well during trending phases. An uptrend could register a prolonged period of overbought conditions, whereas a downtrend could register a prolonged period of oversold conditions (See Figure 8.6).

Figure 8.6: RSI

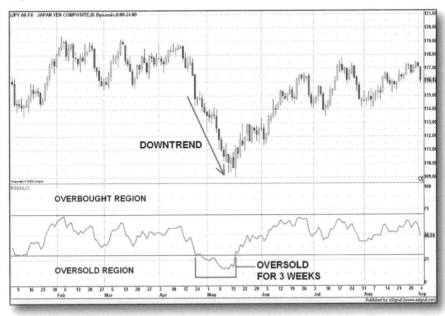

A period of downtrend on the daily chart of USD/JPY corresponds to a three-week oversold condition in RSI. Traders who bought USD/JPY seeing that it was oversold possibly ended up with losses as USD/JPY stayed in the oversold territory for three weeks.

RSI divergence signals

The most useful way of applying the RSI is through its divergence signals. When divergence starts to appear after a directional move, it strongly indicates that a turning point of the current trend is near, and can help you gauge reversal price breakouts. Like MACD, bullish divergence occurs when a currency pair declines to a new low, but the RSI makes a higher low. Bearish divergence is simply the opposite – a currency pair rallies to a new high, but RSI makes a lower high instead (see Figure 8.7).

Figure 8.7: RSI divergence signals

Examples of a bearish divergence and a bullish divergence are shown on this daily chart of AUD/USD. As you can see, being able to identify RSI divergence can help you prepare for a high probability trend reversal.

How does this price-RSI divergence occur?

As you can tell from the RSI's calculation, the average up closes for a period is divided by the average down closes over the same period. This is how a bearish divergence may take place: In an uptrend, a currency pair will advance to higher highs, and result in more average up closes compared to the down closes. Both the price and the RSI will then reach a peak reflecting this. Usually, after an advance, the currency pair tends to take a break and consolidate for a while before deciding the next move. Currency prices may retrace slightly or move sideways during this time. This decline or sideway move in prices will cause the RSI to slope downward from its peak since the number of times the currency pair is up in price divided by the number of times the currency pair is down in price decreases.

When the currency pair later tests or moves slightly higher than its previous high, the RSI will form a lower peak this time compared to its previous peak, since the RSI formula takes into consideration the period of decline and consolidation. This lower peak may signal that the bulls are not as strong as they seem to be, and they could be running out of buying power if no new bulls enter the market. This bearish divergence warns of a potential trend reversal ahead, and if the currency pair is close to touching a support level, a breakout to the downside is more likely to be sustained and successful than short-lived and false. The opposite situation is true for a bullish divergence.

For the Breakout Trading Strategy, using momentum indicators like MACD or the RSI can sometimes provide clues to internal trend weakness since momentum precedes price change. While it may be impossible to predict with 100% accuracy the success of a breakout, as well as the length and duration of the subsequent breakout move, you can make use of these momentum tools to alert you to the possibility of a significant reaction or even a trend reversal breakout of the currency pair.

Identifying the Opportunities

If a trader were to trade every time a currency pair attempts a breakout of a support or resistance level, his or her account balance would look very sorry. Before you implement a breakout trade, detailed analysis of the current technical and market situation must be carried out in order to tilt the odds of success to your side. Trading breakouts can be a very profitable strategy if it is employed sensibly and carefully after thorough analysis.

Where potential breakouts occur

Price breakouts do not just spontaneously take place at any time, although they may be triggered under the influence of sudden forex-related news or comments or unexpected geopolitical events. Breakouts usually occur in zones whereby bulls and bears are engaged in a tumultuous conflict, with one side feeling anxious about defending the zone, and the other group feeling eager to launch a deadly attack. A lot of force and momentum is required to push currency prices beyond their comfort zone, but no one really has the information of how much buying pressure is available or is needed to launch an upside breakout or how much selling pressure is available or needed to start a downward cascade of prices. Such zones of conflict can be found along trendlines, channels, and around price points and after the completion of chart patterns.

We'll now look at trendline and channel breakouts in some more detail.

1. Trendlines

Breakouts frequently occur along trendlines. An up trendline represents points of support, whereas a down trendline represents points of resistance. Hence, when prices break out of these trendlines, it may show that the crowd could be changing the way it thinks and acts. In an uptrend, bulls may become less and less bullish with time, while in a downtrend, bears may become less and less bearish with time.

When currency prices violate the trendline, there are generally two implications for the future course of prices. A trendline breakout could signal a reversal or continuation of trend. In the case of trend continuation, this break may indicate a temporary interruption in the prevailing trend or signal that the trend will continue, but at a slower pace. Since the basic premise of technical analysis is to assume a continuation of a trend unless proved otherwise by technical signals, you should assume that an initial trendline breakout indicates a slower continuation of the current trend.

How can you tell whether it is signalling reversal or consolidation?

You can't really tell from trendline breaks alone, but if you can combine the trendline with other chart patterns – like a head-and-shoulders pattern – you will have a better chance of predicting the outcome of the breakout. If you think it is more likely a consolidation breakout, then set a smaller profit objective. However, if you have other technical or fundamental factors to back up the possibility of a reversal breakout, a larger profit objective may be set, since prices usually tend to move more at the turn of a trend than during a trend continuation. You may even decide to trade multiple lots to stagger-exit your profits at different price levels, but you must adhere to your money management plan, and be aware of the cumulative risks.

Technical execution

1. Is the currency pair approaching a trendline drawn on the hourly or daily chart? Depending on your holding time frame, you may trade a trendline breakout based on the hourly or daily chart.

2. Note the gradient of the trendline.

3. Confirm price momentum with the MACD or RSI. The oscillator should preferably be sloping up strongly before the currency pair attempts an upside breakout, or sloping down strongly before the pair attempts a downside breakout.

4. Check for reversal chart pattern formations on the hourly and daily charts.

5. Wait for the price to close beyond the trendline on an hourly chart.

6. Enter a market or stop entry order once the price moves a few pips past the breakout level.

7. Your stop should be placed according to how long you intend to hold the position for. Those who prefer a tight stop may place it close to the breakout level in the pre-breakout zone. Alternatively, you may place your stop on the other side of the previous intraday range.

8. Your profit target, depending on how long you wish to hold your position open for, could be the next barrier in the form of a trendline or price support or resistance.

2. Channels

A channel defines a technical range between support and resistance levels that a currency pair has traded in, and can span over any period of time. A channel basically consists of two parallel trendlines which can be drawn to encapsulate the price action. A trend channel can be horizontal, looking like a rectangle, or it can be sloping upward or downward.

Prices cannot be trapped forever within the channel, and at some point there will be a trigger, usually fundamental, to set off a burst of price movement beyond the trading range. When currency prices break out of the upper channel, they are generally assumed to continue to move in that upward direction, while a price breakout of the lower channel generally implies a continued price movement in the downward direction.

Trading channel breakouts is a very popular trading technique among traders as the pattern is very easily recognisable; however, being so easily recognisable brings about the same problem of being very likely to be manipulated by strong hands. Since a price breakout of a channel is normally seen as a bullish sign upon an upside breakout, and a bearish sign upon a downside breakout, many traders are expected to place their entry or exit stops just outside both sides of the channel, for they perceive a change of status quo when either of the two boundaries is violated.

In order to maximise the success of the Breakout Trading Strategy, I only trade breakouts that arise from the trendline that defines the underlying trend, that is, I only trade the upside breakout of a descending channel or the downside breakout of an ascending channel. I usually ignore upside breakouts of an ascending channel or the downside breakouts of a descending channel (See Figures 8.8 and 8.9).

Figure 8.8: channel breakouts

In this 60-min chart of GBP/USD, the downside breakout from an ascending channel proved to be more sustained than a prior upside breakout.

Figure 8.9: channel breakouts

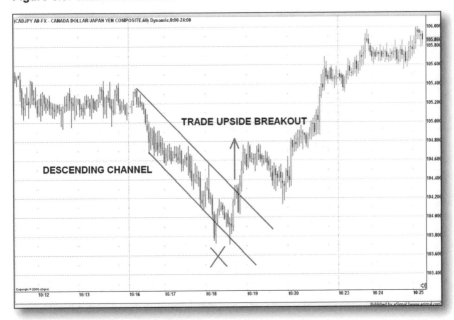

In this 60-min chart of CAD/JPY, the upside breakout from a descending channel proved to be more sustained than a prior downside breakout.

From my observations, sloping channel breakouts that occur in the same direction of the underlying trend based on the trendline, are very likely to suffer from exhaustion moves, and hence are likely to be short-lived and unsustainable. If the subsequent price moves resulting from the same-direction breakout later retraces back toward the channel boundary and bounces off it to close beyond it, then you may join in the trend continuation at that point, but preferably not at the point of breakout.

Another thing to note when trading channel breakouts is the gradient of the channel lines. If the channel lines are steep, then a downside (upside) breakout of an ascending (descending) channel tends to give way to a gentler trendline or channel. When that happens, prices may not move much during the breakout move, as they are more likely to move sideways in a period of consolidation. Personally, I would not trade breakouts from steep channels because the profit objective can be quite small especially if they occur in intraday time frames.

When trading breakouts of a horizontal channel or a rectangle, take note of the pip range of the channel. The tighter the vertical range, the better the chances of a successful breakout. Also, it is more reliable to trade these breakouts if they occur on a minimum hourly time frame. For example, if you spot a channel on an hourly chart that measures 40-50 pips from top to bottom, then the likelihood of a sustained breakout is quite high.

Technical execution

1. Identify a preferably narrow channel formation on an hourly or daily chart, depending on your holding time frame.

2. Confirm price momentum with the MACD or RSI. The oscillator should preferably be sloping up strongly before the currency pair attempts an upside breakout, or sloping down strongly before the pair attempts a downside breakout.

3. If the channel is horizontal and resembles a rectangle, you may trade the breakout on either side of the channel. Enter a market or stop entry order once the price moves a few pips past the breakout level.

4. If the channel is sloping, trade only the downside breakout of an ascending channel or only the upside breakout of a descending channel. Enter a market or stop entry order once the price moves a few pips past the breakout level.

5. Your stop should be placed according to how long you intend to hold the position for. Those who prefer tight stops may place them close to the breakout level in the pre-breakout zone. Alternatively, you may place your stop on the other side of the previous intraday range.

6. Your profit target, depending on how long you want to hold your position open for, could be the projected width of the channel or be time-based.

Remember that you should always assume a trend continuation rather than a trend reversal from a breakout, unless you have evidence – whether from technicals or fundamentals – that point to a reversal outcome. The probability of a trend reversing sharply rather than slowing its pace of movement and then moving sideways is relatively low in the absence of news and/or divergence signals from momentum indicators. Hence, the general rule of thumb is that breakouts from steep channels and trendlines tend to result in price consolidation rather than a reversal. Keeping this tip in mind can save you lots of money and headaches when trading breakouts.

Chart patterns

The most interesting aspect of learning technical analysis must be the thrill of discovering tried and tested chart patterns that purportedly are able to yield predictable price responses – just the sort of magic that technical traders need in order to win in the forex market. Breakouts – whether true or false ones – occur very frequently in chart patterns, as the current situation of supply and demand is likely to change with the completion of a pattern. Chart patterns can be formed over any period of time, ranging from intraday to weekly time frames, but the longer it takes for the pattern to form, the greater the subsequent price movement is likely to be.

Common chart patterns include the head-and-shoulders, double top/bottom, triangles, flags, pennants, diamonds and so on. Chart pattern breakouts refer to currency prices breaking outside of the current price range within the pattern into new price territory, and these breakouts can either signal trend continuation or trend reversal. For example, an upright head-and-shoulders pattern usually alerts the trader to a potential trend reversal if it is found near the end of a mature uptrend, but if the price fails to break out of the neckline, the uptrend may continue from there.

The degree of technical analysis used in the forex market is much higher than that used in other financial markets like stock markets, and hence many forex traders have no problem identifying these common patterns on the currency price charts. Coffee talk among traders could revolve around the discussion of these chart patterns without any difficulty. Chart patterns, especially those that are more easily identified by the majority of the market, hardly do any justice to those who trade their breakouts, since the majority usually can't win from the minority. Just like certain species of deep sea creatures inadvertently invite danger from predators when they emit fluorescent light from the cells of their body against the pitch-black ocean, traders who trade the breakouts of very obvious chart patterns are setting themselves up for possible game manipulation by stronger institutional hands.

Traditional technical analysis books may exalt the reliability of these patterns, but they just do not work as well in the forex market. I have increasingly noticed that in recent times, the first attempt of a price breakout usually results in a failure, the most notorious of all being the head-and-shoulders pattern. As such, I tend to stay away from trading the first breakout attempt from chart patterns.

Filtering False Breakouts

I usually do not trade a price breakout at the first attempt, unless there are other reasons (technicals or market sentiment) to convince me to do so. While most people are more afraid of losing out on a potentially great opportunity than losing their money in a bad trade, I prefer to let the price breakout play out the scene first before deciding on the next move. One way of doing that is to check if the currency price will close beyond the breakout level on the hourly chart.

Focus on an hourly time frame that displays the price actions either in the candlestick or bar format. Language-wise, I will refer to either the candlestick or bar as the candle. If the candle closes beyond the breakout level on the hourly chart, you may then place a short order at least 10 pips below that candle's low for a downside breakout. The opposite is true for an upside breakout – you may open a long position when any subsequent candle exceeds more than 10 pips above that candle's high (see Figure 8.10). This filtering technique only works if there is still more room left for the currency pair to move before it reaches its average daily range.

If the price does go back to the breakout level, you will need to monitor the price action even more attentively as its behaviour around that level could provide you with important clues as to the next price movement. A false breakout is almost certain if the price moves back into the pre-breakout range, but if it is repelled by the breakout level, and does not penetrate past it, there is a higher chance of the price moving in the direction of the breakout.

Figure 8.10: filtering breakouts

Prices broke out of the down trendline on this 60-min chart of USD/JPY, but the breakout was not traded at the first breakout attempt. In accordance to the filtering technique, the long order (that was placed at least 10 pips above the high of the breakout candle) was only triggered many hours later, after a short period of congestion. Subsequently, USD/JPY rallied by more than 70 pips from the long entry point.

Remember that the success of a breakout relies on the second and subsequent waves of traders joining in the breakout, sustaining the breakout like a self-fulfilling prophecy. Let's say in a downside breakout, the price soon returns to the breakout level after penetrating the support. For the breakout not to fail there must be more selling interest from a second wave of traders who see that it is a good opportunity to short at that breakout level in order to overcome the opposing buying interest. This second wave of traders are selling in anticipation of lower currency prices after seeing the bearish technical picture, thus pushing down the currency price from the breakout level of support. The reverse applies to an upside breakout.

If you see that prices are bouncing off that breakout point on the rebound trip, you could place your breakout trade with a limit or market entry order, with a stop placed at least 20 pips on the other side of the breakout level or outside of the day's price range, depending on your risk tolerance. Once the price movement picks up speed in the direction of the original breakout, and breaks below the low (high) of the downside (upside) breakout candle, there is a high probability of the breakout being successful since this new low (high) is another confirmation of a successful breakout.

This way of filtering a fleeting short-lived breakout offers some protection against losses even though like all trading tactics it is not completely fail-proof.

Summary

There are many different outcomes that can be expected when prices attempt breakouts of established levels of support or resistance. A breakout may result in a sustained price move in the direction of the breakout, or may result in failure of the price to sustain a move past the breakout level, or may even generate whipsaw moves that result in losses on both sides of the fence. Before employing the Breakout Trading Strategy, the trader has to closely examine the clues that are present in currency price charts. Compile as many clues as possible so as to filter out potential false breakouts.

Before setting an order to trade breakouts, it is best to make sure that the current market sentiment is in line with the directional bias of your trade. False breakouts can and do occur with little or no warning, even in the most seemingly perfect chart setups, especially when the market is weak. Despite having certain safeguards in place to lead the way towards trading a high probability breakout, there is absolutely no way of ascertaining the definite outcome of a breakout before or when it happens, for a breakout could still fail despite having met some of the criteria. That is why a sensible risk management plan must always be part of any trading strategy.

9:
Strategy 5 –
Decreased
Volatility Breakout

Strategy 5 – Decreased Volatility Breakout

Trading breakouts is undeniably one of the most popular ways of profiting from the forex market, and an earlier chapter has been devoted to the Breakout Trading Strategy. In this chapter, I will discuss one of my favourite subsets of breakout trading – the Decreased Volatility Breakout. While this strategy is similar to the strategy of trading breakouts, it is specific to a certain condition in the forex market.

Pull up any currency price chart and you will notice that currency movements can be quite volatile as they often fluctuate even in the midst of a trending phase, rallying at one moment and declining the next, or vice versa.

Volatility is a measure of the scale of price fluctuations over time. Volatility tends to be high when prices change to a large extent within a short period of time. The reverse is true – volatility tends to be low when prices oscillate more or less close to a certain price level, without deviating much in a short period of time.

It is indeed the volatile nature of the forex market that draws risk-seeking traders and investors to it in search of high profits, for prices have to move by a decent amount in order for profits to be reaped. However, entering the market when prices are experiencing high volatility can be bad for your health – as you face the stress and worry of whether the trade will go your way as prices move up and down sharply.

Instead of merely focusing on the high volatility element of the market, why not concentrate on the periods of decreased volatility in the market?

Yes, it is possible to detect such quiet periods in the often noisy forex market-place.

The Volatility Rollercoaster

There is a tendency for currency prices in the forex market to alternate between periods of low volatility and high volatility, just like the volatility cycle seen in other financial markets. At one time, the market may experience low price volatility, and the next it may experience high volatility, and vice versa. Overly active movements of currency prices may then switch to not moving much at all, maintaining a more or less stable pricing. This recurring pattern has to do with crowd psychology, which is the force behind changes in currency prices. I have mentioned previously the four main stages of a trend:

1. Nascent trend

2. Fully charged trend

3. Aging trend

4. End of trend

At each stage of a trend, there is a different crowd psychology to influence it, and these stages are closely linked to the cycle of volatility in the market.

Stage 1 – Nascent trend

When a currency pair is just starting to trend either on the upside or downside, most market players are still skeptical and cautious about the possible new trend direction during the nascent stage of the trend. Volatility is thus low as both bulls and bears tread carefully.

Stage 2 – Fully charged trend

When the trend progresses to Stage 2, it becomes fully charged and is ready for more action, as there is now new evidence from fundamental data or events that supports the trend direction. Traders who are on the opposite side of the market are caught by surprise, and their vulnerability becomes exposed when the newly introduced information proves them wrong. During this period, a lot of changing positions will take place, causing the price to move more dramatically within that trend period. The new information provides the stamp of approval on the prevailing trend. Traders are now more convinced of the trend direction, favouring a particular currency over another, bringing prices to higher highs in an uptrend or lower lows in a downtrend. Traders who were initially on the wrong side of the market become new converts of the trend, while other traders who have been correct about the trend direction may establish more positions in the direction of the trend. Hence, volatility tends to be high during this stage.

Stage 3 – Aging trend

Stage 3 of the trend sees a period of consolidation as the trend comes close to maturity. Volatility tends to decrease at this stage as the trend momentum becomes exhausted. This is the period where a lot of profit-taking will take place, and appetites of inexperienced traders are satisfied as the more experienced traders get rid of their wares. The trend takes a short break, with both bulls and bears hesitant to make daring moves. Usually such a period of consolidation takes place after the currency prices have moved by a huge amount in the previous period of high volatility, and prices tend to stay relatively tame during this period.

Stage 4 – End of trend

Just like a wild beast cannot remain tamed for too long, the forex market cannot stay apprehensive forever. Sooner or later, some spark – usually derived from economic data or geopolitical events – will trigger sudden reactions from the resting market. High volatility in the forex market will then return with a vengeance as the prevailing trend ends and reverses after new incoming information is revealed about a currency that changes the mass opinion, resulting in a rapid adjustment of prices within a short period of time as market players absorb the new information. Traders scramble desperately to get out of their positions if they have been on the wrong side; many stops get triggered, leading to a sharp follow-through of prices in the reversed direction.

As you can see, even within a trend, currency prices can experience decreased volatility, followed by increased volatility, and vice versa, with an endless cycle of this rollercoaster motion – as crowd psychology tends to be quite predictable.

Decreased volatility can be found during trending or ranging phases, and is especially visible on the price charts prior to the release of certain significant economic news. Traders with open positions in the market are the most vulnerable to unanticipated news during this period of low volatility. However, decreased volatility provides a great opportunity for traders to prepare and profit from an imminent transition from low to high volatility, where gains can be made from unsuspecting players, and that is the basis of the Decreased Volatility Breakout Strategy.

Ways of Measuring Volatility

Even though currency prices seem to move in a very haphazard way, there are several technical indicators which can help you visualise the volatility of currency prices. I will show you two indicators–

1. the moving average, and

2. Bollinger bands

which you can use to gauge the volatility of currency prices.

1. Moving average

A moving average is a simple but very handy indicator to add to your price charts to indicate volatility as well as determining the underlying trend. A moving average attempts to smooth and minimise "noisy data". There are several variations of moving averages: simple, exponential and weighted.

Simple moving average (SMA)

A simple moving average is calculated by adding together the closing prices of a currency pair over certain period of time, and then dividing the total by the number of data points involved. For example, a 20-period simple moving average of say, the EUR/USD, on a daily chart would be calculated by adding the closing prices of the past 20 days and dividing the sum total by 20.

What makes this average "move" is that as new data comes in, it is incorporated into the calculation of the sum total, while the oldest data, which is the first period of the calculation, is dropped from it. In that way, the average changes and adapts to each new period of data even though it is still calculated based on the same number of periods.

Figure 9.1: simple moving averages

There are two different simple moving averages on this daily chart of EUR/USD. Notice how the 100-day SMA tends to be further away from the current price compared to the 20-day SMA. This is because with the 100-day SMA, the closing prices of the last 100 periods are added up and then divided by 100.

Exponential moving average (EMA)

An exponential moving average puts more emphasis on more recent data and less weight on old data in the calculation of the moving average, and is thus perceived by many traders to be more relevant to the current situation.

This is the formula for the exponential moving average:

```
EMA = EMAp + {K * (Price - EMAp)}

where,
EMA   = exponential moving average
EMAp  = the previous period exponential moving average
K     = smoothing constant
Price = current price
K, the smoothing constant, is derived from the time period
selected by the individual according to the formula below:
K     = 2/n+1, where n is the period selected.

The smoothing constant, K, refers to the percentage of
weighting on the current value to be used.
```

Figure 9.2: comparing EMA and SMA

50 EMA

50 SMA

As you can see in this daily chart of GBP/CHF, the exponential moving average has a faster reaction to price changes than the simple moving average, as the EMA places a higher weighting on recent data than on older data.

As the moving average is a lagging indicator, it will react only after prices have moved. When it slopes up, it indicates that prices have been rising, and that the trend is up. The reverse is true; when a moving average slopes downward, it indicates weakness of the currency pair, and that the trend is down. When a moving average is moving sideways, we can deduce that prices are also moving sideways in a period of consolidation (see Figure 9.3). Since prices tend to be more volatile while they are moving up or down, you will see that the moving average will move more wildly when tracking highly volatile price actions.

Decreased volatility is detected when a moving average moves sideways, and looks like a smooth horizontal line. This indicates that the currency pair has settled into a consolidation phase, and the trend has been interrupted, whether temporarily or permanently.

Figure 9.3: exponential moving averages

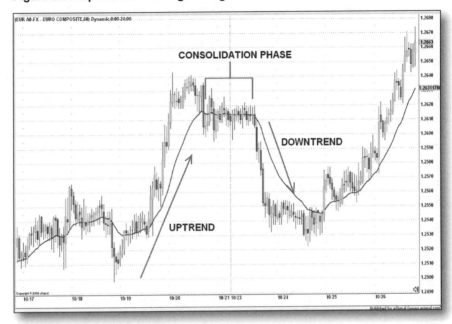

This 60-min chart of EUR/USD shows the 20-period exponential moving average (EMA) trailing the currency prices. As prices rallied in an uptrend, the EMA sloped upward till the point where it began to move sideways as EUR/USD shifted from high to low volatility into a period of consolidation. Later, as prices declined, the EMA sloped downward accordingly.

Regardless of whether you use an exponential or simple moving average, you will find it an interesting indicator of price volatility as it smoothes the numerous price fluctuations into a more visibly pleasing format, which tells you at a quick glance the volatility picture of the currency pair.

One thing to note is that as a *lagging indicator*, the moving average, however, may not be a very timely volatility gauge, and may still be sloping upward or downward even when prices are already showing decreased volatility and are moving sideways.

2. Bollinger bands

Another technical tool that traders can use to measure volatility of a currency pair is the Bollinger bands. According to default settings found in most charting software, the Bollinger bands are two lines which are plotted two standard deviations of a 20-period time horizon above and below a moving average. The upper band represents +2 standard deviations, the lower band -2 standard deviations, and the centre line is a 20-period simple moving average.

You may notice from Figure 9.4 that as USD/JPY becomes more volatile, the bands increase in width, and when the pair becomes less volatile, the band width becomes narrower as both the upper and lower bands converge towards the centre line. This relationship between the band width and price volatility stems from the fact that standard deviation measures volatility. Increased volatility is represented by a widening band width, whereas decreased volatility is represented by a narrowing band width.

Figure 9.4: Bollinger bands

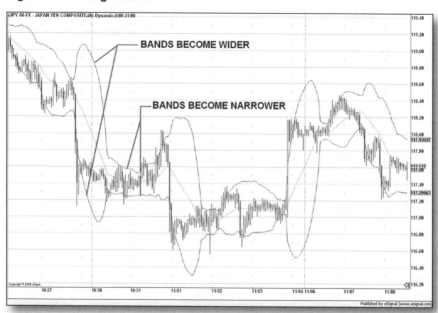

This 60-min chart of USD/JPY shows that as prices become more volatile, Bollinger bands become wider, and as prices become less volatile, the bands shrink in width.

Triangles

Triangles are one of the best depictions of decreasing price volatility in the currency price charts, and are relatively common in charts. Through triangle formations, you can take advantage of the decreasing price volatility in the forex market; they allow you to bank in and ride on a potentially high momentum move that is likely to occur after a period of decreasing volatility. All triangles show decreasing price volatility in action, and when a particular type of triangle has been identified by the trader, a high-probability trade may be in sight when technicals are coupled with the current market sentiment.

Keep in mind that the Decreased Volatility Breakout Strategy is based on the assumption that when a currency pair, which has been moving in tight ranges, is finally ready for a transition to high volatility, it is likely to gain enough momentum to power a sustained move of prices in that direction of breakout.

Identifying the particular type of triangle

Triangles are generally continuation patterns although they can also be reversal patterns, depending on the different types of triangles and whether they occur in an existing uptrend or downtrend. There are basically three types of triangles:

1. ascending,

2. descending, and

3. symmetrical.

These triangles are also sometimes called *wedges*.

Decreased price volatility can be represented by all these three types of triangles, and it pays to know how to identify each one of them so that you can employ the Decreased Volatility Breakout Strategy when the opportunity arises.

1. Ascending triangles

When you see an ascending triangle on the chart, it is generally a bullish signal, even though it can either be a continuation or reversal pattern. An ascending triangle can be easily identified by its upward slope. This upward sloping trendline, which connects the higher price lows, creates the lower boundary of the triangle. The upper boundary, which is roughly horizontal, represents the resistance level, and should connect at least two price points.

The crowd psychology behind the ascending triangle is as follows: Every time the currency price goes up to a certain level (that forms the resistance), there are sellers (of the currency pair) who are convinced about selling at that high, thus pushing the price down each time that particular level is tested. On the other hand, when prices retreat from the high on the way down, there are buyers (of the currency pair) who believe very strongly that the currency pair should rise based on their own reasons, and thus bid the price higher than the previous low, forming the upward slope of the triangle. The triangle is formed when these two lines converge at a point, which forms the apex. Even though the bulls and bears show disagreement, they themselves are not too eager to go long or short respectively, which explains why volatility is decreasing. Usually this hesitancy is a common reaction before the release of new data.

The appearance of an ascending triangle should prepare you for an upside breakout from the resistance level (see Figure 9.5). Although it is impossible to predict with razor-sharp accuracy that that will be the true outcome of the eventual breakout, the probability is quite high. Breakouts tend to occur in the middle or in the final one-third of the triangle formation, measuring from the start of the triangle to the tip.

Figure 9.5: ascending triangle

USD/JPY successfully broke above the upper boundary of the ascending triangle on a daily chart in a classic fashion. In this case, since the ascending triangle appeared after a downtrend, the triangle served as a reversal pattern.

This is what usually happens during an upside breakout: Once prices break out of the resistance level of an ascending triangle upon some trigger, sellers (of the currency pair) who have been shorting below that level are caught in the wrong direction, and become desperate to close their shorts by buying, hence bidding prices higher, fuelling the upside price move even more.

The general guideline is that if the ascending triangle is formed during an existing uptrend, it is seen as an uptrend continuation pattern. But if it is formed during an existing downtrend, it acts as a bullish reversal pattern.

That said, in the actual market, prices can move whichever way they want, without being bound by theories of how they should move. Sometimes, prices can also break out from below the ascending triangle successfully, tricking the majority with a downside breakout, catching them unaware (See Figure 9.6).

Figure 9.6: ascending triangle with breakout on the downside

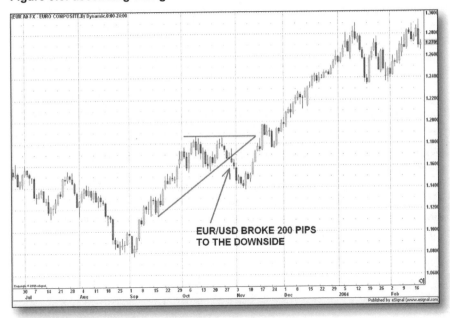

An ascending triangle was formed in the midst of an uptrend on a daily chart of EUR/USD. But instead of breaking out from the top of the triangle, EUR/USD broke below the triangle in a 200-pip move over the next few days.

2. Descending triangles

A descending triangle works the opposite way of an ascending triangle, and is generally viewed as a bearish formation even though it can either be a continuation or reversal pattern.

A descending triangle can be easily identified by its downward slope, which forms the upper boundary of the triangle. This down trendline is drawn by connecting the lower price highs. The horizontal lower boundary of the triangle represents the support level, and should connect at least two price points.

The crowd psychology behind the descending triangle is as follows. Every time the currency price goes down to a certain level (that forms the support), there are buyers (of the currency pair) who are stubborn about holding up that level with firm bidding, thus pushing the price up each time that particular level is tested. Bears, however, are quite anxious to sell as they feel that the currency price should fall over time. Thus, when prices bounce off the support level, bears take the opportunity to short again, with each offer getting lower and lower than the previous offer. This is reflected by the downward sloping trendline. As with ascending triangles, bulls and bears face a skirmish amidst decreasing volatility of the market, with both camps not feeling too confident of the next market move, this can easily occur prior to a significant news release.

Spotting a descending triangle allows you to be prepared for a possible downside breakout from the support level, especially when a currency pair is trending downward (see Figure 9.7).

Similarly, prices tend to break out in the middle or in the final third of the triangle formation, measuring from the start of the triangle to the tip. When the support line is violated, many of those long positions which have been placed above that level soon get stopped when prices reach their stops which have been placed below the horizontal support line. This domino effect causes prices to go down even lower, thus fulfilling a sustained downside breakout.

Figure 9.7: descending triangle

In a classic move GBP/USD successfully broke below the lower boundary of the descending triangle on a daily chart. In this case, since the descending triangle appeared in the midst of a downtrend, the triangle served as a continuation pattern.

If the descending triangle is formed during an existing downtrend, it tends to give off even more bearish vibes than if it is formed during an uptrend, because you should always assume the continuation of the prevailing trend unless you have reversal signals in the form of technicals or a turnaround of market sentiment. Despite the general rule of thumb, prices can also sometimes break out from above the descending triangle successfully in a burst of bullish momentum.

3. Symmetrical triangles

Another variety of triangle is the symmetrical triangle, which has some resemblance to a wedge pattern. A symmetrical triangle consists of two converging trendlines that join a series of lower highs and higher lows; it is differentiated from sloping triangles by the absence of a horizontal line (see Figure 9.8).

The lower highs reflect the mildly bearish conviction of sellers (of the currency pair) as they are willing to accept less and less over time, while the higher lows are formed when buyers (of the currency pair) are willing to pay a bit more to get a piece of the action. It is in this way that the volatility slowly shrinks such that prices become gradually trapped within the narrow confines of the triangle prison. As with other sloping triangles, breakouts usually occur in the middle or final third of the triangle.

Although you should assume that an eventual breakout of this pattern is resolved in the underlying trend direction, either an upside or a downside breakout can happen (see Figure 9.8). There is no way to predict its future breakout direction until one of the lines is penetrated. Hence, a symmetrical triangle tends to be less reliable compared to an ascending or descending triangle.

Figure 9.8: symmetrical triangle

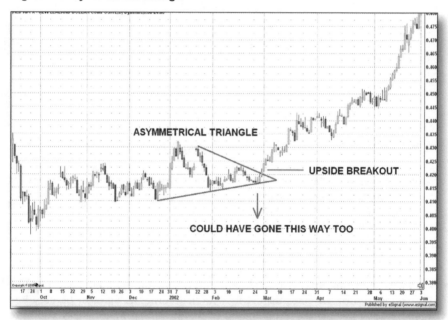

This daily chart of NZD/USD shows a symmetrical triangle. Even though the breakout could have occurred on either side of the triangle, NZD/USD broke above the triangle instead.

Technical execution of the strategy

Once you have identified the type of triangle on either the daily or weekly chart, the next thing to do is to prepare for a breakout in either direction, even though each different type of triangle has its own directional bias, with the exception of a symmetrical triangle. When trading triangle breakouts, it is preferable to ignore any first breakout attempt, regardless of whether the breakout is to the upside or the downside. Scenarios A and B are applicable if you have identified ascending or descending triangles, while Scenario C is meant for breakouts from symmetrical triangles.

Scenario A

The second breakout attempt is in the direction that is highly expected of the particular type of triangle. In other words, the second attempt is an upside breakout of an ascending triangle, or a downside breakout of a descending triangle (see Figure 9.9). This breakout could signal either continuation of the underlying trend or a trend reversal.

Figure 9.9: Scenario A

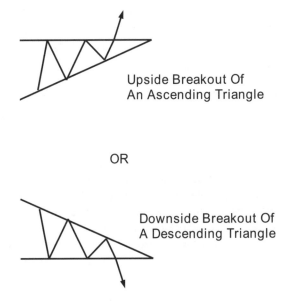

Upside Breakout Of
An Ascending Triangle

OR

Downside Breakout Of
A Descending Triangle

Long order for ascending triangle

1. Make sure that each side of the triangle has already been touched at least twice.

2. Ignore any first breakout attempt.

3. Place a stop-buy entry order at least 10 pips above the horizontal resistance level to capture a subsequent potential upside breakout.

4. Place a stop-loss order at least 10 pips beyond the opposite side of the triangle to guard against false breakouts. If the stop is too wide according to your money

management rules, the position size for the trade should be reduced. For those who prefer tighter stops, the stop-loss may also be placed at least 10 pips below the horizontal resistance level.

5. Profit target should be set according to your own trading time-frame.

Short order for descending triangle

1. Make sure that each side of the triangle has already been touched at least twice.

2. Ignore any first breakout attempt.

3. Place a stop-sell entry order at least 10 pips below the horizontal support level to capture a subsequent potential downside breakout.

4. Place a stop-loss order at least 10 pips beyond the opposite side of the triangle to guard against false breakouts. If the stop is too wide according to your money management rules, the position size for the trade should be reduced. For those who prefer tighter stops, the stop-loss may also be placed at least 10 pips above the horizontal support level.

5. Set profit target according to your own trading time-frame.

Scenario B

The second breakout attempt is in the opposite direction that is to be expected of the particular type of triangle. In other words, the second attempt is a downside breakout of an ascending triangle, or an upside breakout of a descending triangle (see Figure 9.10). Position size for trades executed in this scenario should ideally be halved so as to mitigate the risk of a false breakout since the breakout direction is contrary to the one that is more favoured by the particular triangle type.

Figure 9.10: Scenario B

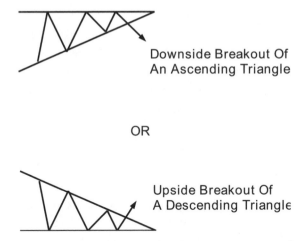

Downside Breakout Of
An Ascending Triangle

OR

Upside Breakout Of
A Descending Triangle

Short order for ascending triangle

1. Make sure that each side of the triangle has already been touched at least twice.

2. Ignore any first breakout attempt.

3. Place a stop-sell entry order at least 10 pips below the upward sloping line to capture a subsequent potential downside breakout. Reduce position size by half for this trade.

4. Place a stop-loss order at least 10 pips beyond the opposite side of the triangle to guard against false breakouts. If the stop is too wide according to your money management rules, the position size for the trade should be further reduced. For those who prefer tighter stops, the stop-loss may also be placed at least 10 pips away from the breakout point in the triangle zone.

5. Set profit target according to your own trading time-frame.

Long order for descending triangle

1. Make sure that each side of the triangle has already been touched at least twice.

2. Ignore any first breakout attempt.

3. Place a stop-buy entry order at least 10 pips above the downward sloping line

to capture a subsequent potential upside breakout. Reduce position size by half for this trade.

4. Place a stop-loss order at least 10 pips beyond the opposite side of the triangle to guard against false breakouts. If the stop is too wide according to your money management rules, the position size for the trade should be further reduced. For those who prefer tighter stops, the stop-loss may also be placed at least 10 pips away from the breakout point in the triangle zone.

5. Set profit target according to your own trading time-frame.

Scenario C

This shall apply to breakouts from symmetrical triangles. Usually, there is an equal probability of an upside or downside breakout occurring from a symmetrical triangle, especially if both trendlines of the triangle start from similar points in time, thus making both trendlines equally valid.

Long entry

1. Make sure that each side of the triangle has already been touched at least twice.

2. Ignore any first breakout attempt.

3. Place a stop-buy entry order at least 10 pips above the downward sloping line to capture a subsequent potential upside breakout.

4. Place a stop-loss order at least 10 pips beyond the opposite side of the triangle to guard against false breakouts. If the stop is too wide according to your money management rules, the position size for the trade should be reduced. For those who prefer tighter stops, the stop-loss may also be placed at least 10 pips away from the breakout point in the triangle zone.

5. Set profit target according to your own trading time-frame.

Short entry

1. Make sure that each side of the triangle has already been touched at least twice.

2. Ignore any first breakout attempt.

3. Place a stop-sell entry order at least 10 pips below the upward sloping line to capture a subsequent potential downside breakout.

4. Place a stop-loss order at least 10 pips beyond the opposite side of the triangle to guard against false breakouts. If the stop is too wide according to your money

management rules, the position size for the trade should be reduced. For those who prefer tighter stops, the stop-loss may also be placed at least 10 pips away from the breakout point in the triangle zone.

5. Set profit target according to your own trading time-frame.

Further strategy enhancement

When trading triangle breakouts, it is advantageous to consider other pieces of information so that you can better pinpoint a high-probability trade setup. Besides the triangle formation, decreased volatility can also be detected with the exponential moving average (EMA) and the Bollinger band indicator. The EMA should ideally be moving sideways, and the Bollinger band indicator should show a narrowing of band width. However, their inherent tardiness means that their technical agreement is not a prerequisite for trading this strategy, even though an additional confirmation from either of these tools should reinforce your judgment of the current situation.

Summary

Currency prices experience a periodic cycle of varying volatility, from low to high volatility, and vice versa. Such phases of decreased volatility are often resting breaks for currency pairs particularly after a sharp volatile move, whereby bulls and bears hold a temporary truce and think about their next course of action. The longer the amount of time a currency pair experiences decreased volatility, the more powerful the subsequent breakout move tends to be. This is because when bulls and bears are jolted out of their sleep in the restful period, many will find themselves in the wrong direction as prices break out, and will exit their existing positions, moving prices further and further away from the decreased volatility zone, which could be in the form of triangles.

The Decreased Volatility Breakout Strategy works better when it is implemented on daily or weekly charts, rather than intraday charts even though periods of decreased volatility can also be found in shorter time frames. And as with trading breakouts of any kind, put together as much evidence as you can to support a particular breakout direction so as to minimise the risks of trading false breakouts.

10:
Strategy 6 –
Carry Trade

Strategy 6 – Carry Trade

Is it possible to earn some passive income while you hold certain currency positions over a period of time? The spot forex market offers just that opportunity. The Carry Trade Strategy is a popular way of trading the global forex market, and is a strategy highly favoured by large financial institutions such as hedge funds, pension funds and banks. What makes carry trades so desirable is the possibility of earning interest, which is a unique aspect that traders – both big and small alike – can take advantage of.

All currencies in the world have interest rates attached to them, and these rates are decided by each country's central bank. For example, the Federal Reserve Bank in the US determines the country's interest rates while the Bank of England sets the United Kingdom's interest rates. Since each country sets its own interest rate, countries – or, rather, their currencies – are bound to have varying interest rates. Some countries may have relatively higher interest rates while others may have relatively lower rates. How can traders exploit the fact that some currencies have much higher interest rates than others? Let me introduce you to the concept of a carry trade.

What Is A Carry Trade?

A carry trade is a long-term fundamental trading strategy that involves the selling of a certain currency with a relatively low interest rate, and using the funds to buy a currency which gives a higher interest rate, with the hope that the high-interest-rate currency will appreciate against the low-interest-rate-currency. When these positions are held overnight, carry traders are paid interest on the currency they are long in, and must pay interest on the currency they are shorting. The interesting aspect of this strategy is that the investor or trader is able to gain the difference between these two interest rates, known as the interest rate differential or spread, which can be a hefty amount when leveraged.

A Basic Carry Trade Strategy

1. Buy a currency with a high interest rate, and

2. Sell a currency with a low interest rate

Currencies and interest rates

*   Currencies with typically **high** interest rates: GBP, NZD, AUD, CAD

*   Currencies with typically **low** interest rates: JPY, CHF

The Japanese yen and the Swiss franc tend to be on the selling side of the carry trade due to their traditionally low interest rates. Such low-interest-rate currencies are known as funding currencies since they are used to fund the purchase of high interest rate currencies such as the British pound, the New Zealand dollar or the Australian dollar which tend to have high interest rates.

Example: carry trade

Here is an example of a carry trade. Let's say the Japanese yen has an interest rate of 0.25%, and the New Zealand dollar gives an interest rate of 7.25%. Since the New Zealand dollar has a higher interest rate than the Japanese yen, a trader who wishes to profit from a carry trade may buy the New Zealand dollar and sell the Japanese yen at the same time. An annualised profit of around 7% (7.25% - 0.25%) may be reaped from the carry trade if no leverage is used. This return is based on the assumption that the exchange rate between the New Zealand dollar and Japanese yen remains unchanged throughout the holding period of one year. If that carry trade is carried out with a 10 times leverage, it will increase the unleveraged 7% annualised return to a huge 70% annualised return.

The conventional notation of currency pairs is such that JPY and CHF tend to be the counter currency while GBP, NZD and AUD tend to be the base currency in a currency pair. Hence, traders who are interested in carry trades will long currency pairs like GBP/JPY, AUD/JPY or NZD/CHF, effectively buying the first currency in each pair (which also tends to be the higher-yielding currency) and simultaneously selling the second currency in the pair (which tends to be the lower-yielding currency). Since they are trading these currency pairs in the long direction, they will want the base or high-yielding currencies to strengthen in value against the counter or low-yielding currencies.

More Money Will Follow The Money

Global institutional investors, such as hedge funds and banks, are constantly on the lookout for the highest rate of return on their funds, and have no qualms about shifting their money around, in the global sense. This act of shifting huge amounts of money into high-yielding assets lays the foundation of the carry trade, since a carry trade is all about borrowing money at low interest rates and then using the funds to purchase higher yielding financial instruments from elsewhere, which can include bonds or even cash itself.

For quite some time, institutional or individual investors have been able to enjoy and exploit the large interest rate spread between US and Japan. Investors were drawn to borrowing the Japanese yen at near zero percent interest rate and using the money to buy US treasury bonds which gave them a much higher rate of return. The conversion of Japanese yen into US dollars for the purchase of the US bonds has resulted into a form of carry trade even though the asset may not be in cash because these assets are nonetheless denominated in the high-interest-rate currency. So it does not matter if investors are moving their money into bonds, currencies or other instruments, because it is ultimately cash that is changing hands.

This conversion from one currency to another is significant if it is done on a large scale as an increased demand for that high-interest-rate currency will cause that currency to appreciate against the low-yielding currency. Usually, birds of the same feather will flock together, with money attracting more money to the same place as other investors follow suit. Forex traders, sensing this snowballing effect, will then execute carry trades in the currency market, with the hope that there will be a continued demand for the high-yielding currency as they can then profit from the interest spread as well as from capital appreciation.

Factors Supportive Of Carry Trades

Good economic and political conditions of the high-yielding currency

When it comes to deciding where to invest their money, investors will not only assess the rate of return, but also the economic conditions and political stability of the country which holds the assets. Generally speaking, developed countries that offer relatively high interest rates are those which tend to experience decent economic growth and expansion, which may in turn attract more foreign investment into their country. An economy that is doing reasonably well will more likely be able to pay high interest rates to investors. However, it is not just the more developed countries that may offer high interest rates; many emerging economies may do so as well, simply because they tend to experience higher inflation. These are generally not countries where most investors will park their money due to the high level of economic instability.

Political stability is also another aspect that investors are concerned with because a politically stable country will provide a good framework for trade and investment. Adverse economic and/or political conditions could have a negative impact on foreign investment in the country, and may cause investors to move their assets out and convert the high-yielding currency into their local currencies, thus resulting in depreciation in exchange rates of the carry pair.

Widening interest rate gap

The wider the difference in interest rates between the two currencies in a pair, the higher the interest that will be paid to traders who long the carry pair (with the high-yielding currency as the first currency in the pair) over a period of time. And the higher the interest fees that will be paid, the more it will attract other traders or investors to enter carry trades, thereby potentially pushing up the value of the high-yielding currency further as demand for it increases.

On the other hand, a narrowing interest rate gap between the two currencies will cause traders and investors to lose interest in holding their carry trades and discourage more people from joining in the carry trades as the interest fees paid out will decrease. Such a scenario can occur when interest rate hikes are expected to take place in the country of the low-yielding currency, thereby lifting the currency from the current low interest rate, or when interest rates are expected to be cut in the country of the high-yielding currency.

So as a rule of thumb, the wider the interest rate gap exists between the two currencies, the higher the likelihood of a profitable long-term carry trade.

Risks Involved In Carry Trade

The biggest risk in the Carry Trade Strategy is the uncertainty of future exchange rate fluctuations.

For a carry trade to work, the high-yielding currency must rise, or at the very least remain steady, against the low-yielding one over a period of time. A depreciation of the high-yielding currency can cause carry traders to lose money, as they are betting on an unchanged or a rising exchange rate of the currency pair, and this decline can even erase any gains earned from the interest.

For example, if you go long on a currency pair like NZD/JPY as a carry trade, you expect and want the New Zealand dollar to appreciate in value or at least remain unchanged versus the Japanese yen for however long you intend to hold your position for. If NZD/JPY goes up, you will stand to gain not just from the interest spread, but also from capital appreciation. The risk then is for the carry trade pair to decline more in percentage than what you would gain from the interest fees.

You must understand the fundamentals

If you are thinking of employing the Carry Trade Strategy, you must first understand the fundamental factors that are supportive of carry trades, and be confident that the high-yielding currency will continue to rise or stay unchanged against the low-yielding currency over a period of time. Should market sentiment reverse and change due to economic, monetary or political conditions, carry traders may decide to liquidate their long positions (by selling), perceiving that the high-yielding currency would drop in value, and thus harm their long trades. This unwinding can come about quickly and without much warning, and can usually last for quite some time (months or even years) especially if overall perception towards the currencies in the carry pair is changed drastically based on major fundamental changes. Another reason for the possible prolonged unwinding of carry trades is that not all carry trades will unwind at the same time.

NZD/JPY cross

For example, in 2005, the NZD/JPY cross was one of the more popular currency pairs to carry trade as it offered a wide interest rate spread. At that time, with New Zealand's interest rates standing at 7.25% and Japan's interest rates remaining at 0%, a trader buying the NZD/JPY could make 725 basis points from yield alone. If a 10 times leverage had been applied to this carry trade, it would have yielded a 72.5% annual return from the rate gap alone, and that was in addition to capital appreciation of the pair itself.

Anyway, NZD/JPY was in an overall uptrend in 2005, which was good news for carry traders as they not only made on the substantial interest spread (if leveraged), they also gained from the rising strength of NZD/JPY. However, near the end of

2005, things started to turn sour for carry traders. There were market rumblings about the possibility of Japan discarding the Zero Interest Rate Policy, and investors worldwide feared that the Japanese central bank was going to raise interest rates sometime in 2006. That resulted in a six-month decline of NZD/JPY as carry traders and investors closed their longs (see Figure 10.1).

Figure 10.1: NZD/JPY carry trade unwinding

This daily chart of NZD/JPY shows the steady uptrend of the currency pair from the start of 2005 till the end of 2005 during which the pair rallied 1600 pips in all, and its rapid decline from December 2005 till May 2006, during which the pair plunged by 1900 pips due to a major shift in market sentiment.

NZD/JPY was not the only currency pair to suffer the consequences of carry trade unwinding. USD/JPY, being another hugely popular carry trade pair, also experienced a severe and sharp decline from December 2005 till May 2006, when the Bank of Japan hinted at raising interest rates in Japan (see Figure 10.2).

Figure 10.2: USD/JPY carry trade unwinding

This daily chart of USD/JPY shows the steady uptrend of the currency pair from the start of 2005 till the end of 2005, and the effect of carry trade unwinding from December 2005 till May 2006.

Points of Entry

Once you have evaluated the fundamental factors that are supportive of a profitable long-term carry trade, the next thing to do is to look at the technical picture of the carry pair that you are interested in (or you can check out the technical outlook first before assessing the fundamental factors).

Open up the daily or weekly chart of the pair and see how it has been moving over the intermediate and long-term time frame. Has it been moving in an uptrend, downtrend or sideways? If the overall fundamental picture looks supportive of a carry trade, you may position yourself for a possible uptrend by buying near price or trendline support levels or by trading upside breakouts. Since carry pairs could be trending upward for quite a while, they make good candidates for trading trendline or price support bounces.

Exercise extra caution when you see that the currency pair has been trending south over the intermediate and long-term time frame because that clearly shows a gradual liquidation of long positions by carry traders and investors. In that case, the Carry Trade Strategy is not recommended for that currency pair at that time.

Other Considerations

While the Carry Trade Strategy has the potential means to maximise your trading profits, there are a few things to keep in mind when planning a carry trade.

Holding time frame

Traders must be aware that this strategy is not meant for short-term trading, as time is instrumental in the realisation of decent profits. I would advise a minimum holding time frame of at least three months for a carry trade, provided that the market sentiment does not turn adversely against the preferred direction of the carry trade. Reasonable (i.e. not tight) stops must be put in place if your carry trades are to endure short-term market fluctuations without being stopped out.

Leverage

Institutional players tend to execute the Carry Trade Strategy with some amount of leverage. Leverage has the power to transform single-digit returns into super-powered double-digit ones. Independent traders may also apply leverage (preferably not more than 10 times) for carry trades so as to potentially increase their rate of return.

But, of course, leverage works both ways. As much as it can be a highly desirable tool to increase your profits, it can also be a highly destructive weapon that is capable of magnifying your losses. New traders can often get too carried away with the prospect of being able to use high leverage that they overlook the importance of money management. Use a moderate amount of leverage with caution as excessive leverage has the capacity to diminish your trading capital in a short time.

Summary

A carry trade is meant as a long-term strategy, and should only be considered by traders who are comfortable leaving their positions open over a few months to a year or so.

Both fundamental and technical factors must be taken into consideration in order to increase the probability of success of this strategy.

While interest may be gained, a carry trade is subjected to the risk of depreciation of the currency which has the higher interest rate relative to the other currency in the pair. Therefore, besides looking for currency pairs which offer a wide interest rate differential between the two currencies, you also need to assess the directional bias (based on economic and political conditions) of the currency pair you are considering to carry trade, and to determine the potential for the higher-yielding currency to appreciate against the low-yielding one. Thus, it is important for carry traders to be aware of what central bank officials may say or hint about the outlook of their country's economy and monetary policy.

11:
Strategy 7 –
News Straddling

Strategy 7 – News Straddling

In this era where information can be an extremely powerful and strategic asset, whether to individuals or corporations, and information equals money, especially for a trader, shutting yourself off from news can be suicidal. The forex market is extremely sensitive to the flow of news that is related to it, and major short-term currency moves are almost always preceded by changes in fundamental views influenced by the news. Traders around the world make a living by processing and translating information into money. Financial news services providers know how important news is to the forex market players, and charge a premium for it. It is not uncommon to get hundreds of headlines of news that are potentially relevant to forex trading from any news service provider on an average trading day.

Traders, especially those who day trade the forex market, require the latest up-to-the-second news updates so as to facilitate their trading decisions which have to be made at lightning speed. They mostly make use of online financial newswire services such as Dow Jones Newswires, Bloomberg and Reuters, which display the latest financial news on their computer monitors. Since the speed of news dissemination is very important to traders, many opt for these online instant news services rather than depending on daily newspapers like the Wall Street Journal or the Financial Times which carry stale news that is of little use to traders.

The Importance of News

News that is of great importance to forex traders is generally related to a country's economic, monetary and political situations, and socio-political events that are happening around the world, with special attention on the Middle-East and isolated countries in Asia like North Korea.

The underlying reason why news is so important to forex trading is that each new piece of information can potentially alter the trader's perceptions of the current and/or future situation relating to the outlook of certain currency pairs. When people's opinions or beliefs are changed, they tend to act on these changed perceptions through buying or selling actions in the forex market. Based on the news, these traders will be preparing to cover their existing positions or to initiate new positions. A trader's action is based on the expectation that there will be a follow-through in prices when other traders see and interpret the same news in a similar way that he or she has, and adopt the same directional bias as the trader as a result.

News is a very important catalyst of short-term price movements because of the expected impact it has on other market players, and this is in a way an anticipatory reaction on the part of the trader as he or she assumes that other traders will be affected by the news as well.

If the news happens to be bullish, say for the US dollar, traders who react the fastest will be among the first to buy the US dollar, followed soon by other traders who may react slower to the news or are waiting for certain technical criteria to be met before jumping onto the bandwagon. And there will be those who join in the buying frenzy at a later stage when they get hold of the delayed news in the morning newspapers or from their brokers. This progressive entry of US dollar bulls over a period of time is what sustains the upward move of the US dollar against another currency, with the USD exchange rate going higher against other currencies. The reverse is true for bearish news, traders will sell because they know that others will soon be selling, thus pushing the USD exchange rate down. This is based on the assumption that since other traders will be getting the same pieces of news, they will be also tend to be affected the same way.

Publicly released news is disseminated to the various newswires. Any trader with access to these wires can tap into the information given out, and react accordingly in the forex market. However, institutional players do get information that retail traders don't, as they get privy access to order book information in their computer systems, and may also know something that others don't through their personal contacts in the industry.

In the world of forex trading, there are no rules or restrictions against insider trading! Anyone who possesses information that is known only to a select few can and do trade that information in the forex market. Sometimes, such news may give an unfair advantage to these institutional players, but at other times, this isolated news access may not translate into real market action if other players do not have that information.

Think of it this way: The forex market is dependent on news, for if there is no news, there would be little or negligible price movements in the market. Even if currencies may move according to the technicals sometimes, the technicals have been established previously by news or expectations of future news, and so the influence of news on currency prices is inevitable and inescapable.

Market's Reaction to News

Market reaction to news is staggered

The market's reaction to news is specific as it depends on both the type of medium that the news is transmitted on and the type of news that is being released. Most active traders get their market information from electronic market news services, all of which relay information to the traders' computer screens at almost exactly the same time as soon as market events occur, with very slight or no discernible delay between the actual time of release and the display of news. Other less active traders may rely on daily market commentaries written by analysts, and published on websites or in newspapers as they feel they have no need to for real-time news. The market's reaction can thus be staggered, ranging from an immediate reaction (within the first second) from those who receive real-time news, to a more delayed reaction from those who obtain the same news hours or even days later.

It is not uncommon for the forex economic calendar to be packed with an average of twenty economic news releases per trading day. The market reacts differently to different news; some news may produce little or no reaction at all.

Due to the overflowing amount of forex-related information invading the newswires and other media, you have to be very selective of what news to focus on as the market reacts to a varying degree in relation to the type of news that is released. During times of scheduled news releases, currency prices adjust very rapidly to the market's perceptions of the released data or comments relating to the data. Since prices react very fast to news, it does not really matter whether the information is accurate or not, as precious time cannot be spared to double-check the facts.

The market reacts to the "what" of the news, not the "why". For example, currency prices will move as the market reacts to the better than expected unemployment figure. The market will not have time to be concerned about why the unemployment rate is better this month compared to the previous month. If a trader were to ponder why a particular piece of economic data is good or bad, instead of taking advantage of the situation, he or she might as well be an analyst, not a trader, as traders do not usually need to concern themselves with the "why".

The discounting effect

Very often, I get traders asking me why a particular currency has rallied despite that country's negative economic figures, or why the currency has declined despite positive news (see the following chart). To a newcomer, that cause and effect may seem a bit bewildering and confusing, but that is perfectly understandable. When there is good economic news about a country, say, the United Kingdom, commonsense says that the British pound should go up accordingly as investors and traders get bullish on the economy; if the country shows signs of economic weakness, the pound should go down accordingly to reflect the underlying fundamentals of the country. The reason as to why a particular currency has gone up despite poor economic data from that country, (or has declined despite positive economic data) can be attributed to the discounting mechanism of the forex market.

Figure 11.1: the British Pound drops despite positive economic data

GBP/USD fell after the release of positive UK labour data on 16 May 2007, which showed that unemployment, as measured by the claimant count, fell for the seventh time in a row, to 2.8% in April from 2.9% in March, which was the lowest level of unemployment since November 2005.

The market's in-built discounting mechanism is formed by the anticipatory reaction of traders as they take into consideration current expectations of the future in their present trading decisions. If they think that Japan will suffer from rising oil prices in the near or long term, they will be bearish on the Japanese yen and go short now, thus pushing down the currency. But if traders have a positive view about the Japanese economy, they will be bullish on the yen and go long now, hence pushing up the currency price. It is this manner of anticipating the future and incorporating those expectations into the present exchange rates that causes the market to discount the implications of future possible developments. In this way, currency prices integrate the market's present expectations of the future. This is somewhat similar to the common market saying: "Buy on the rumour, sell on the news".

Are expectations being met?

Even before actual economic data is released, the market already has its own estimate of what the figures could be based on the media's interview of analysts and economists, as well as the internal work of analysts in the major trading institutions such as banks or funds. For example, the consensus for an upcoming US consumer confidence survey is for the index to show a worse figure compared to the previous month. And way before that same survey result is released, the market has already priced that expectation into the exchange rate of, say the EUR/USD, which has been rallying due to the resulting weak USD sentiment. Now, what will really move the EUR/USD at the point of that consumer confidence release is the amount of deviation between expectations and the actual news.

If the released figure comes out just as expected by the market, it is already old news to traders, as they have already factored that into the currency price beforehand. Such anticipated news or economic data does not cause any surprise in the market as they merely confirm prior expectations. In fact, the release of anticipated news or data often can cause the currency price to move in the opposite direction of where the market has largely positioned itself before the news. So, for example, if the US consumer confidence headline figure turns out to be almost identical to the market's expectations, EUR/USD may even end up declining, with USD strengthening even in the face of a negative consumer confidence number. This contrarian market reaction is the result of traders who have gone long on the EUR/USD closing their positions and taking profits upon the news release. Thus, the lack of any deviation of expectations from the actual news or data can either cause a currency pair to move sideways or to move in the opposite direction as the status quo remains, and there is no shift of expectations from the news itself.

The explosive market reaction

What will really move the market in a huge and dramatic way is when there is a large deviation between expectations and the actual news or data release. An unanticipated news or outcome of a data release that contradicts the prevailing market consensus will trigger a big move. Let's say a certain figure is expected for the US payrolls, and the actual number turns out to be less than the expected figure, the US dollar is likely to fall against another currency upon the news release (see the following chart). This new and unexpected piece of information will cause a big shift in traders' mindsets, and prompt them to re-adjust their existing positions or to open new positions in line with the US fundamentals.

Figure 11.2: reaction to data outcome

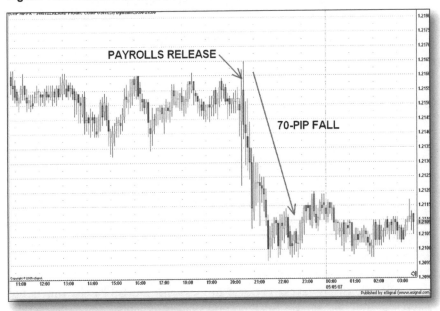

USD/CHF fell 70 pips in one hour following the release of weak US payrolls, which showed a gain of only 88,000 jobs compared to an expected 110,000 gain.

Since many forex players tend to pre-empt what might happen and adjust the current prices to suit that mindset, the market will thus react more substantially to news that contradicts the market's expectations, giving rise to significant moves in the market.

Now that you have a better idea of how important news is to the movement of currency prices, and the various market reactions to news, the next step is to exploit that knowledge with the News Straddling Strategy.

Identifying the Opportunities

Trading news can be a very profitable trading technique if you know when and how to enter the market.

Single out market-moving news

There can easily be at least 15 to 20 economic daily data releases relating to the eight major currencies in the world (which are namely, USD, EUR, GBP, JPY, CHF, CAD, AUD and NZD).

Indeed, the opportunities to trade news are plenty almost every day, but who has the time to trade every piece of news that comes out? The forex market actually does its own filtering of news and is generally most influenced by US economic news.

Although the forex market also reacts to economic news from other countries, these news releases usually take a backseat to those that are US-based. This is not surprising given that the US has the world's largest economy, and is the world's major trading partner. Therefore the possible changing state of the US economy is of utmost importance and relevance to other countries' economies as America's fate is closely linked to that of many other countries. That is why US economic news announcements have the greatest potential to influence other countries' economies and their respective currencies. In fact, with at least 80% of all foreign exchange trades being traded in terms of the US dollar, it would be to your advantage to focus mainly on US-based economic news.

Since economic news relating to the US tends to have the most impact on the overall currency market, and have the biggest hand in deciding how currencies should close relative to the USD by the end of a 24-hour period, they are the most widely anticipated by the majority of the market.

An initial part of the News Straddling Strategy is to pick out the various market-moving news announcements that can have a big impact on the forex market.

Major economic data releases

Here is a general list of economic news that is of significance to the market, especially if they relate to large economies such as the US or the Euro zone (they are not listed in the order of importance):

1. Unemployment

2. Interest rate decision

3. Inflation

4. Consumer confidence

5. Trade balance

6. Home sales

7. Industrial production

8. Retail sales

9. Manufacturing

10. Business sentiment

Some news announcements are more important than others, depending on which country the news is related to, the other economic news that is released at the same time, as well as depending on the current hot theme that keeps most financial journalists on their toes, and gets them talking. You can usually get a sense of this by catching up on news reports or analysis distributed by electronic or traditional news media. The theme could change from week to week, or from month to month, or from year to year, depending on the state of the country's economy. For example, trade balance data in the current month may be more important than the unemployment rate, and in the following year, interest rate decisions may become more important than the trade balance figure.

Note the schedule of news releases

Many economic reports are released once every month. If you want to trade these news releases, it is essential to note the dates of the release on your trading calendar.

Other than the dates, you should also take note of the time of release. These news releases are usually announced around 1200 or 1300 GMT, which is morning in the US, and while the European markets are still open.

You can check the release schedule of these news items ahead of time by going to the website of the department of the specific country that is responsible for it.

The following table shows a number of major economic releases relating to the US, and their respective departments in charge of it.

Table 11.1: Major US economic releases

Data	Released by	URL
Non-Farm Payrolls	Released by the US Department of Labour – Bureau of Labor Statistics	www.bls.gov
Personal Consumption Expenditure	Released by the US Department of Commerce- Bureau of Economic Analysis	www.bea.gov (Under "Personal Income And Outlays")
US Trade Balance	Jointly released by the Bureau of the Census and Bureau of Economic Analysis	www.bea.gov (Under "U.S. International Trade in Goods and Services")
Treasury International Capital Flow	Released by the US Department of the Treasury	www.ustreas.gov
FOMC Rate Decision and Minutes of Meeting	Announced by the Federal Reserve	www.federalreserve.gov/ FOMC/default.htm#calendars

Which currency pair to trade for this strategy?

Before you trade news, you first need to decide which currency pair you are going to trade. Since the News Straddling Strategy is an intraday strategy that capitalises on the relatively high amount of volatility that is usually generated with news announcements, it may be more advantageous to focus on the more volatile currency pairs. Because the most market-moving news generally relate to the US, the strategy should be applied on currency pairs that involve the USD. Hence, some good candidates for this strategy are the majors: EUR/USD, USD/JPY, GBP/USD and USD/CHF.

I have found that certain currency pairs among the majors tend to respond better than others when it comes to trading major news releases. Out of the four majors, EUR/USD, USD/CHF and GBP/USD tend to be better candidates than USD/JPY as the European markets are normally still open during the time of US news releases, whereas Asian markets which usually trade the yen are already closed. The following charts illustrate the responses of these four currency pairs within the first 30 minutes of the US trade balance report's release. Of these four, GBP/USD moved the most in terms of pips with a 60-pip move; USD/CHF and the EUR/USD moved nearly the same amount with a move of 45 pips, and the USD/JPY moved the least with a move of 30 pips.

Figure 11.3: GBP/USD

Figure 11.4: USD/CHF

Figure 11.5: EUR/USD

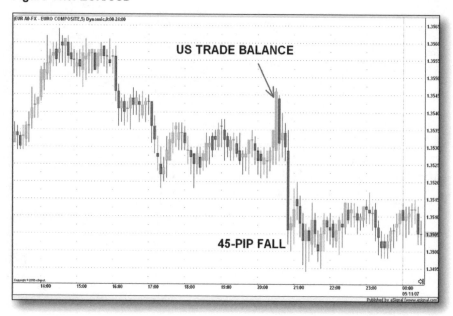

Figure 11.6: USD/JPY

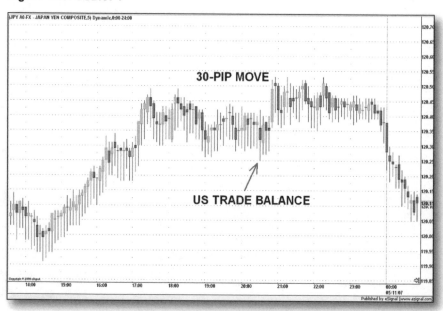

Technical considerations

The News Straddling Strategy is only employed upon the release of significant scheduled news. The assumption is that moderate to very high price volatility can be expected during such news, and that we can profit from the resulting sharp market moves.

This strategy does not require you to interpret the released data before placing your trade, as the time taken to do so would be money gone in a very fast-moving market. The strategy requires very nimble and fast entry and exit execution because currency prices usually respond very quickly in a knee-jerk reaction to a move in one direction, and may correct themselves very quickly.

For this strategy, I recommend that you concentrate mainly on the EUR/USD pair, based on its superior liquidity compared to the other currency majors, but if you have had no major problems trading the other currency pairs during news, then by all means trade those.

My rule for the News Straddling Strategy is this:

Either we enter at the price we want or we stay out of the market completely.

This strict condition is pivotal to the maximising of profits with this strategy, as you will soon see.

Market-makers and slippage

When trading news, the risk of slippage can be very high, as currency prices tend to move very fast during such highly volatile market conditions. Slippage occurs when the price at which you intend to enter or exit the market is different from your actual transacted price, and that is the biggest problem with placing stop or market entry orders. These orders do get filled, but possibly at a completely different price from the one that you have specified. Sometimes, these entry orders may even get filled past your profit target or stop-loss, which means that when both your entry and profit limit or stop-loss orders are filled, you would be left with an immediate net loss.

Many market makers will wait till after the big move before they fill your entry order, and will many times fill your stop-loss or profit-limit first before filling your entry order with wide slippage. It is a sly trick which many of them use in order to make an immediate profit by filling your positions with a negative spread.

For example, you have set your long entry stop for USD/JPY at 117.00 and your profit-limit at 117.30. The market-maker may first fill your profit limit at 117.30, then fill your long entry stop at 117.40 with a 40-pip slippage, resulting in your position having a net realised loss – even though your trade would have been profitable if filled at the prices you wanted.

The market maker may also fill your stop-loss order first if the trade goes against you, and then fill your entry order with slippage after that so as to widen their profit. For example, you have set your long entry stop at 117.00 and your stop-loss at 116.80. The market-maker could first fill your stop-loss at 116.80, then fill your long entry stop at 117.30 with a 30-pip slippage, resulting in your position suffering a 50-pip loss instead of the planned 20-pip loss due to slippage.

The bottom line is: the larger the slippage you experience, the more you stand to lose, and the more some market-makers stand to profit from your trades. As an individual trader, it is necessary to know that during news some market-makers may add slippage to any of your orders in order to increase their own profits. They will merely place your entry orders as pending, and often till you get stopped out or your profit limit is reached.

Many traders readily accept the risk of slippage as one of the realities of news trading, without much concern that slippage can eat up a huge chunk of profits, and affect their overall profit/loss. But it does not have to be this way. One way of circumventing this problem is through the use of the stop-limit entry order, which I highly recommend for the News Straddling Strategy.

Type of entry order to be used

A stop-limit order is basically an order which becomes a limit order once the currency reaches the designated stop price. Only after the specified stop price has been reached or exceeded will the stop-limit order instruct the broker to buy or sell at a specific price or better, which is essentially when the stop-limit order becomes a limit order.

The main advantage of using a stop-limit order with the News Straddling Strategy is that the trader can decide ahead of time the price at which the trade will get executed, but the stop-limit order may not get filled at all in a fast-moving market. The price may not stay within the limit range long enough for the order to get executed, or there may not be enough supply or demand at that price which it is to be filled. By using a stop-limit order, we are instructing that the entry price is either filled at limit or better, or not executed at all. It is much preferable that the position is not opened at all if we are not able to trade at the entry price that we want, rather than to risk slippage with other types of orders, which is in line with the rule of the strategy.

However, some brokers do not accept stop-limit orders in their systems. If the broker that you are currently using does not allow this function, you have basically three options: The first is to place just a simple stop entry order, and accept the risk of slippage; second is to stay out of the market during news; and the third is to switch to another broker which allows the placing of stop-limit orders.

Let's take a look at how you can apply the News Straddling Strategy.

The Approach

The straddling approach is conceptually similar to a channel breakout strategy.

Very often, a horizontal price channel is formed prior to the release of important news, and may be identified on an intraday chart like the 5-minute or 60-minute chart.

First of all, draw a lower line connecting a minimum of two low points which form the support base, and draw an upper parallel line connecting a minimum of two high points which form the resistance. These boundaries then form a channel on your chart. The channel should be relatively narrow, spanning not more than 40 pips in width preferably (see Figure 11.7). A channel basically encapsulates the delicate balance of power between both the bulls and bears. This makes sense as neither bulls nor bears tend to be over-enthusiastic about their bias before an important news release.

Thus, the presence of a narrow price channel prior to the news release will set the stage for the application of this strategy.

Figure 11.7: a price channel forming before news

A 35-pip channel has formed on a 5-min chart of EUR/USD on the day of the Non-Farm Payrolls (NFP) release on 6 October 2006. The narrower a channel is prior to a major news release, the more powerful the breakout is likely to be.

Trade entry

Once you have identified and drawn a narrow horizontal channel on the 5-minute chart of a currency pair, say, the EUR/USD, monitor the price action for at least 20 minutes prior to the important news release. The prices should ideally continue to move within the channel boundaries. As you may have guessed, there are bound to be many entry and stop-loss orders placed just past these support and resistance levels, with many new traders anticipating prices to break out either to the upside or downside with a lot of borrowed momentum from the news release.

In order to catch a potentially sharp breakout move, a stop-limit long entry order is placed a few pips above the resistance line of the channel, and a stop-limit short entry order is placed a few pips below the support line of the channel. Sometimes, prices may even pierce through either channel line by about 10-20 pips before the news release. In that case, place your stop-limit entry orders a few pips below that pierced low and a few pips above that pierced high (see Figure 11.8). Use *stop-limit* orders instead of just stop orders to enter your positions. Recall that the rule of this strategy is that we either enter at the price we want or we stay out completely. Place your entry orders not more than a few minutes before the news release.

Figure 11.8: entry levels

This is the 5-min chart of EUR/USD on the day of the Non-Farm Payrolls (NFP) release on 6 October 2006. Note that in this case, the long entry was triggered first upon the data release, but ended with a loss, while the short entry was triggered soon after, and ended with a profit.

There are some traders who prefer to place an entry order only in the direction of the underlying trend of the past few days. For example, they will only go long if it is an uptrend, and only go short if it is a downtrend. Actually, it is really up to you to modify the entry criteria based on your own preferences and risk tolerance. You can either place orders to capture either direction of a breakout move, or an order to capture only one direction of the resulting move.

The price will, on most occasions, break out of the price channel, either above or below it upon the news release, and one of your positions will be opened. You could keep the other entry order open just in case the prices stage a failed breakout, and then reverse to break out from the other channel boundary.

Trade exit

Each stop-limit entry order must be accompanied with a specified stop-loss and profit-limit orders. For a long entry, a stop sell order is placed at least 20 pips below the resistance line, and for a short entry, a stop sell order is placed at least 20 pips above the support line. The assumption is that a successful price breakout should continue past the breakout level, without returning to the pre-breakout price zone. For those traders who have a greater risk appetite, stop-loss orders could also be placed at the same price of the other entry order, such that when the first trade gets stopped out, a new reverse position will be opened to capture the potential breakout from the opposite side of the channel.

The initial profit objective could be approximately equivalent to the width of the channel. So if the channel is about 30 pips wide, aim for an initial objective of around 30 pips (see Figure 11.9). A staggered profit-taking can also be considered. You can set an initial profit objective for half of your total lot size, and set a wider profit objective for the rest of the position, which could be calculated to be about twice the width of the channel. Thus, for a channel that is 30 pips wide, the wider objective can be set around 60 pips. You can also experiment with trailing stops for part of your order or other ways of staggering your profit targets.

Figure 11.9: entry levels

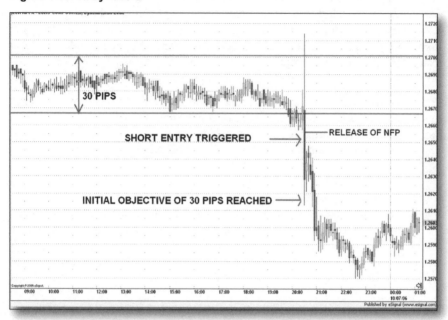

The initial profit objective of 30 pips, which was set based on the channel width, was achieved within a few minutes after the short entry was triggered.

Summary

I have provided only some examples of news which you can trade using the News Straddling Strategy, but this strategy is not limited to only these news releases, it can also apply to other news which does not concern the US. There is such a huge selection of events that occur every month which you can take advantage of to make some good profits. Thus, it is useful to keep track of what news and events are the most talked-about and anticipated in the forex market. If certain themes keep rearing their heads in analysis or commentary reports, then you should be aware of any economic data or speeches relating to these themes for they are very likely to have a significant impact on certain currency pairs. News which at the moment is seen as market-moving could have less impact over time, depending on the economic condition of the country they relate to.

The News Straddling Strategy enables traders to take advantage of important events and to profit from them, without needing to rely on any in-house analysts or economists to say what will happen to currency prices if the actual number comes in how many points more or less than the consensus. Hence, time is not wasted in deciphering whether the news is bullish or bearish, as the core of this strategy is to get in and out of the market quickly without slippage. As with all the other strategies, there is always room for you to modify and customise this strategy to suit your personal trading style and preference.

12:
Appendices

Appendices

Forex Glossary

appreciation
A currency is said to appreciate when it strengthens in price in response to market demand.

arbitrage
Taking advantage of prices in different – but related – markets by the purchase or sale of an instrument and the simultaneous taking of an equal and opposite position in a related market to profit from small price differentials.

ask (offer) price
The price at which the market is prepared to sell a specific currency in a contract. At this price, the trader can buy the base currency. In the quotation, it is shown on the right side of the quotation. For example, if USD/CHF is quoted as 1.2400/04, the ask price is 1.2404, and this means you can buy one US dollar for 1.2404 Swiss francs.

bar chart
A type of chart which consists of four significant points: the high and the low prices, which form the vertical bar, the opening price, which is marked with a little horizontal line to the left of the bar, and the closing price, which is marked with a little horizontal line to the right of the bar.

base currency
The first currency in a currency pair. It shows how much the base currency is worth as measured against the second currency. For example, if the USD/JPY exchange rate is 118.00, then US$1 is worth ¥118.00. In the forex markets, the US Dollar is usually the base currency for quotes, meaning that quotes are expressed as a unit of $1 USD per the other currency quoted in the pair. The main exceptions to this rule are the Euro, the British Pound, the Australian Dollar and the New Zealand Dollar.

basis point
One hundredth of a percent.

bear market
A market distinguished by a prolonged period of declining prices accompanied with widespread pessimism.

bid price
The bid is the price at which the market is prepared to buy a specific currency. At this price, the trader can sell the base currency. It is shown on the left side of the quotation. For example, in the quote EUR/USD 1.3000/03, the bid price is 1.3000. This means that you can sell one Euro for 1.3000 US dollars.

bid/ask spread
The difference between the bid and offer price. For example, if the EUR/USD price is 1.3000/03 then the spread is 0.0003.

book
The summary of currency positions held by a dealer, desk, or room. A total of the assets and liabilities.

broker
An individual or firm that acts as an intermediary, putting together buyers and sellers for a fee or commission. In contrast, a *dealer* commits capital and takes one side of a position, hoping to earn a spread (profit) by closing out the position in a subsequent trade with another party.

Bretton Woods Agreement of 1944
An agreement that established fixed foreign exchange rates for major currencies, provided for central bank intervention in the currency markets, and pegged the price of gold at US $35 per ounce. This agreement governed currency relationships until 1971, when President Nixon overturned the Bretton Woods agreement and established a floating exchange rate system for the major currencies. Before its breakdown, the agreement was useful in maintaining order and accomplishing common objectives among the states that created it.

bucket shop
A brokerage enterprise which books (i.e., takes the opposite side of) a customer's order without actually having it executed on an exchange.

bull market
A market distinguished by a prolonged period of rising prices. Opposite of bear market.

Cable
Trader jargon for the British Pound Sterling, referring to the GBP/USD pair. Term began due to the fact that the rate was originally transmitted via a transatlantic cable starting in the mid 1800s.

candlestick chart
A chart that indicates the trading range for the day as well as the opening and closing price. If the open price is higher than the close price, the rectangle between the open and close price is shaded. If the close price is higher than the open price, that area of the chart is not shaded.

capital markets
Markets for medium to long term investment (usually over 1 year). These tradable instruments are more international than the money market (i.e. Government Bonds and Eurobonds).

central bank
A government or quasi-governmental organisation that manages a country's monetary policy and prints a nation's currency. For example, the US central bank is the Federal Reserve, others include the ECB, BOE, BOJ.

charting
The use of graphs and charts in the technical analysis of markets to plot trends of price movements, average movements of price, volume of trading and open interest.

chartist
An individual who uses charts to interpret historical data to find trends and predict future movements. Also known as a *technical trader*.

clearing house
An adjunct to, or division of, a commodity exchange through which transactions executed on the floor of the exchange are settled. Also charged with assuring the proper conduct of the exchange's delivery procedures and the adequate financing of the trading.

closed position
Exposures in forex that no longer exist. The process to close a position is to sell or buy a certain amount of currency to offset an equal amount of the open position. This will *square* the position.

collateral
Something given to secure a loan or as a guarantee of performance.

commission
A transaction fee charged by a broker.

Commodity Futures Trading Commission (CFTC)
The federal agency created by Congress in 1975 to regulate futures trading and protect participants against manipulation and fraud, through its administration of the Commodities Exchange Act.

contract
The standard unit of trading.

counter currency
The second listed currency in a currency pair.

counterparty
One of the participants in a financial transaction.

counter-trend trading
In technical analysis, the method by which a trader takes a position contrary to the current market direction in anticipation of a change in that direction.

country risk
Risk associated with a cross-border transaction, including but not limited to legal and political conditions.

cross rates
Rates between two currencies, neither of which is the US Dollar.

currency
Any form of money issued by a government or central bank and used as legal tender and a basis for trade.

currency pair
The two currencies that make up a foreign exchange rate. For example, USD/CHF.

currency risk
The probability of an adverse change in exchange rates.

currency swap
Contract which commits two counter-parties to exchange streams of interest payments in different currencies for an agreed period of time and to exchange principal amounts in different currencies at a pre-agreed exchange rate at maturity.

day trading
Opening and closing positions within the same trading session.

dealer
An individual or firm that acts as a principal or counterpart to a transaction. Principals take one side of a position, hoping to earn a spread (profit) by closing out the position in a subsequent trade with another party. In contrast, a broker is an individual or firm that acts as an intermediary, putting together buyers and sellers for a fee or commission.

deficit
A negative balance of trade or payments.

delivery
A forex trade where both sides make and take actual delivery of the currencies traded.

depreciation
A fall in the value of a currency due to market forces.

devaluation
The deliberate downward adjustment of a currency's price, normally by official announcement.

drawdown
The magnitude of a decline in account value, either in percentage or dollar terms, as measured from peak to subsequent trough. For example, if a trader's account increased in value from $10,000 to $20,000, then dropped to $15,000, then increased again to $25,000, that trader would have had a maximum drawdown of $5,000 (incurred when the account declined from $20,000 to $15,000) even though that trader's account was never in a loss position from inception.

economic indicator
A statistic that indicates current economic growth and stability issued by the government or a non-government institution. Some examples include Gross Domestic Product (GDP), employment rates, trade deficits, industrial production, and business inventories.

efficient market
A market in which all information is instantaneously assimilated and reflected in the trading price.

Euro
The currency of the European Monetary Union (EMU). A replacement for the European Currency Unit (ECU).

European Central Bank (ECB)
The central bank for the new European Monetary Union.

European Monetary Union (EMU)
EMU is the agreement among the participating member states of the European Union to adopt a single hard currency and monetary system. The European Council agreed to name this single European currency the *Euro*. On January 1, 1999, the currency exchange rates of the eleven participating member states became permanently fixed, marking the beginning of the third and final phase of the EMU.

exotic currency
A currency with little liquidity and limited dealing, which is neither a major or minor currency.

fast market
Rapid movement in a market caused by strong interest by buyers and/or sellers. Under such circumstances, price levels may be omitted and bid and offer quotations may occur too rapidly to be fully reported.

Federal Deposit Insurance Corporation (FDIC)
The regulatory agency responsible for administering bank depository insurance in the United States.

Federal Open Market Committee (FOMC)
The committee that sets money supply targets in the United States, which tend to be implemented through Fed Fund interest rates and so on.

Federal Reserve (Fed)
The central bank for the United States.

fill or kill order
An order which demands immediate execution or cancellation.

fixed exchange rate
Official rate set by monetary authorities. Often the fixed exchange rate permits fluctuation within a band.

flat/square
Dealer jargon used to describe a position that has been completely reversed. For example, you bought $200,000 then sold $200,000, thus creating a neutral (flat) position.

flexible exchange rate
Exchange rates with a fixed parity against one or more currencies with frequent revaluation's. A form of managed float.

floating exchange rate
An exchange rate where the value is determined by market forces. Even floating currencies are subject to intervention by the monetary authorities; when such activity is frequent the float is known as a dirty float.

foreign exchange (forex or FX)
The simultaneous buying of one currency and selling of another.

foreign exchange swap
Transaction which involves the actual exchange of two currencies (principal amount only) on a specific date at a rate agreed at the time of the conclusion of the contract (short leg), at a date further in the future at a rate agreed at the time of the contract (the long leg).

forward outright
A foreign exchange deal with a maturity beyond the spot delivery date.

forward spread
Refers to the forward premium or discount that the forward price trades at. The forward price is calculated with the spot price, interest rate differential, and days to delivery.

fundamental analysis
Analysis of economic and political information with the objective of determining future movements in a financial market.

futures commission merchant (FCM)
Individuals, associations, partnerships, corporations and trusts that solicit or accept orders for the purchase or sale of any commodity for future delivery on or subject to the rules of any contract market and that accept payment from or extend credit to those whose orders are accepted.

futures contract
A standardised, transferable, exchange-traded contract that requires delivery of a commodity, bond, currency, or stock index, at a specified price, on a specified future date.

FX
Abbreviation for foreign exchange.

G7
The seven leading industrial countries: US, Germany, Japan, France, UK, Canada, Italy.

going long
The purchase of a stock, commodity, or currency for investment or speculation.

going short
The selling of a currency or instrument not owned by the seller.

good-till-cancelled (GTC)
An order to buy or sell at a specified price. The GTC will remain in place until executed or cancelled.

Gross Domestic Product
Total value of a country's output, income or expenditure produced within the country's physical borders.

Gross National Product
Gross domestic product plus income earned from investment or work abroad.

hedge
A position or combination of positions that reduces the risk of your primary position.

inflation
An economic condition whereby prices for consumer goods rise, eroding purchasing power.

initial margin
The initial deposit of collateral required to enter into a position as a guarantee on future performance.

interbank rates
The foreign exchange rates at which large international banks quote other large international banks.

International Monetary Market (IMM)
Part of the Chicago Mercantile Exchange that lists a number of currency and financial futures.

intervention
Action by a central bank to effect the value of its currency by entering the market. Concerted intervention refers to action by a number of central banks to control exchange rates.

leading indicators
Statistics that are considered to predict future economic activity. Examples are Unemployment, Consumer Price Index, Producer Price Index, Retail Sales, Personal Income, Prime Rate, Discount Rate, and Federal Funds Rate.

leverage (also called margin)
The ratio of the amount used in a transaction to the required security deposit.

limit order
An order with restrictions on the maximum price to be paid or the minimum price to be received.

liquidity
The ability of a market to accept large transaction with minimal to no impact on price stability.

London Inter-Bank Offered Rate (LIBOR)
Banks use LIBOR when borrowing from another bank.

long position
A position that appreciates in value if market prices increase. When the base currency in the pair is bought, the position is said to be long.

lot
A unit to measure the size of the deal.

managed float
When the monetary authorities intervene regularly in the market to stabilise the rates or to aim the exchange rate in a required direction.

margin
The required equity that an investor must deposit to collateralise a position.

margin call
A requirement from a broker or dealer for additional funds or other collateral to bring the margin up to a required level to guarantee performance on a position that has moved against the customer.

market correction
In technical analysis, a small reversal in prices following a significant trending period.

market maker
A dealer who supplies prices and is prepared to buy or sell at those stated bid and ask prices. A market maker runs a *trading book*.

market risk
Exposure to changes in market prices.

mark-to-market
Process of re-valuing all open positions with the current market prices. These new values then determine margin requirements.

momentum
In technical analysis, the relative change in price over a specific time interval. Often equated with speed or velocity and considered in terms of relative strength.

money markets
Refers to investments that are short-term (i.e. under one year) and whose participants include banks and other financial institutions. Examples include Deposits, Certificates of Deposit, Repurchase Agreements, Overnight Index Swaps and Commercial Paper. Short-term investments are generally considered safe and highly liquid.

offer (ask)
The rate at which a dealer is willing to sell a currency.

one cancels other order (OCO)
A contingent order where the execution of one part of the order automatically cancels the other part.

online trading
The increasingly popular activity of buying and selling currencies, stocks, options, futures, derivatives and so on through online (commonly internet) trading platforms, which are usually a broker's proprietary software.

open position
An active trade with corresponding unrealised profit or loss, which has not been offset by an equal and opposite deal.

over the counter (OTC)
Used to describe any transaction that is not conducted over an exchange.

overnight position
A trade that remains open until the next business day.

pip (or points)
The term used in currency market to represent the smallest incremental move an exchange rate can make. Normally one basis point (0.0001 in the case of EUR/USD, GBD/USD, USD/CHF and .01 in the case of USD/JPY).

political risk
Exposure to changes in governmental policy which will have an adverse effect on an investor's position.

position
A position is a trading view expressed by buying or selling. It can also refer to the amount of a currency either owned or owed by an investor.

price transparency
Describes quotes to which every market participant has equal access.

profit /loss (or p/l, or gain/loss)
The actual realised gain or loss resulting from trading activities on closed positions, plus the theoretical unrealised gain or loss on open positions that have been mark-to-market.

profit taking
The unwinding of a position to realise profits.

pyramiding
The use of profits on existing positions as margin to increase the size of the position, normally in successively smaller increments.

Rally
A recovery in price after a period of decline.

range
The difference between the highest and lowest price of a currency recorded during a given trading session.

rate
The price of one currency in terms of another currency.

resistance
A term used in technical analysis indicating a specific price level at which analysis concludes people will sell.

retracement
A reversal within a major price trend.

reversal
A change of direction in prices.

risk
Exposure to uncertain change, most often used with a negative connotation of adverse change.

risk capital
The amount of money that one can afford to invest, which, if lost would not affect one's standard of living.

risk management
The employment of financial analysis and trading techniques to reduce and/or control exposure to various types of risk.

risk/reward ratio
The relationship between the probability of loss and profit. This ratio is often used as a basis for trade selection or comparison.

roll-over
Process whereby the settlement of a deal is rolled forward to another value date. The cost of this process is based on the interest rate differential of the two currencies.

round turn (or round trip)
Buying and selling of a specified amount of currency, basically meaning one completed trade.

scalping
The practice of trading in and out of the market on very small price fluctuations. A person who engages in this practice is known as a scalper.

settlement date
The date upon which foreign exchange contracts settle.

short position
An investment position that benefits from a decline in market price. When the base currency in the pair is sold, the position is said to be short.

slippage
The difference in price between what the screen quote indicates and the actual price that gets executed on the trading platform. For example, if the quote shows a bid price of 1.2400 and the trading platform actually executes the trade at 1.2402, there would be 2 pips of slippage – the difference between the signal price and actual execution price.

spread
The difference between the bid and offer prices.

square
Purchase and sales are in balance and thus the dealer has no open position.

squeeze
A market situation in which the lack of supply tends to force shorts to cover their positions by offset at higher prices.

stop loss order
An order to automatically liquidate an open position when a particular price is reached, either above or below the price that prevailed when the order was given. Often used to minimise exposure to losses if the market moves against a trader's position.

support levels
A technique used in technical analysis that indicates a specific price ceiling and floor at which a given exchange rate will automatically correct itself.

swissy
Market slang for Swiss Franc.

technical analysis
An effort to forecast prices by analyzing market data, for example through historical price trends and averages, volumes, open interest, etc.

tick
A minimum change in price, up or down.

tomorrow next (tom/next)
Simultaneous buying and selling of a currency for delivery the following day.

trader
A merchant involved in cash commodities or a professional speculator who trades for his own account.

transaction
The entry or liquidation of a trade.

trend
The general direction, either upward or downward, in which prices have been moving.

trendline
In charting, a line drawn across the bottom or top of a price chart indicating the direction or trend of price movement. If up, the trendline is bullish; if down, it is bearish.

two-way quotation
When a dealer quotes both buying and selling rates for foreign exchange transactions.

unrealised gain/loss
The theoretical gain or loss on open positions valued at current market rates, as determined by the broker in its sole discretion. Unrealised Gains/Losses become Profits/Losses when position is closed.

uptick rule
In the United States, a regulation which states that a security may not be sold short unless the trade prior to the short sale was at a price lower than the price at which the short sale is executed.

value date
The date that both parties of a transaction agree to exchange payments.

volatility (vol)
A statistical measure of a market's price fluctuations over time.

whipsaw
Slang for a condition of a highly volatile market where a sharp price movement is quickly followed by a sharp reversal.

yard
Slang for a billion.

Currency Codes

A table of standard currency codes.

Place	Currency	Code Alphabetic	Numeric
AFGHANISTAN	Afghani	AFN	971
ALBANIA	Lek	ALL	008
ALGERIA	Algerian Dinar	DZD	012
AMERICAN SAMOA	US Dollar	USD	840
ANDORRA	Euro	EUR	978
ANGOLA	Kwanza	AOA	973
ANGUILLA	East Caribbean Dollar	XCD	951
ANTARCTICA	No universal currency		
ANTIGUA AND BARBUDA	East Caribbean Dollar	XCD	951
ARGENTINA	Argentine Peso	ARS	032
ARMENIA	Armenian Dram	AMD	051
ARUBA	Aruban Guilder	AWG	533
AUSTRALIA	Australian Dollar	AUD	036
AUSTRIA	Euro	EUR	978
AZERBAIJAN	Azerbaijanian Manat	AZN	944
BAHAMAS	Bahamian Dollar	BSD	044
BAHRAIN	Bahraini Dinar	BHD	048
BANGLADESH	Taka	BDT	050
BARBADOS	Barbados Dollar	BBD	052
BELARUS	Belarussian Ruble	BYR	974
BELGIUM	Euro	EUR	978
BELIZE	Belize Dollar	BZD	084
BHUTAN	Indian Rupee	INR	356
	Ngultrum	BTN	064
BOLIVIA	Boliviano	BOB	068
	Mvdol	BOV	984
BOSNIA & HERZEGOVINA	Convertible Marks	BAM	977
BOTSWANA	Pula	BWP	072
BOUVET ISLAND	Norwegian Krone	NOK	578
BRAZIL	Brazilian Real	BRL	986
BRITISH INDIAN OCEAN TERRITORY	US Dollar	USD	840
BRUNEI DARUSSALAM	Brunei Dollar	BND	096
BULGARIA	Bulgarian Lev	BGN	975
BURUNDI	Burundi Franc	BIF	108
CAMBODIA	Riel	KHR	116
CANADA	Canadian Dollar	CAD	124

CAPE VERDE	Cape Verde Escudo	CVE	132
CAYMAN ISLANDS	Cayman Islands Dollar	KYD	136
CHILE	Chilean Peso	CLP	CLF
	Unidades de formento	152	990
CHINA	Yuan Renminbi	CNY	156
CHRISTMAS ISLAND	Australian Dollar	AUD	036
COCOS (KEELING) ISLANDS	Australian Dollar	AUD	036
COLOMBIA	Colombian Peso	COP	COU
	Unidad de Valor Real	170	970
COMOROS	Comoro Franc	KMF	174
CONGO, THE DEMOCRATIC REPUBLIC OF	Franc Congolais	CDF	976
COOK ISLANDS	New Zealand Dollar	NZD	554
COSTA RICA	Costa Rican Colon	CRC	188
CROATIA	Croatian Kuna	HRK	191
CUBA	Cuban Peso	CUP	192
CYPRUS	Cyprus Pound	CYP	196
CZECH REPUBLIC	Czech Koruna	CZK	203
DENMARK	Danish Krone	DKK	208
DJIBOUTI	Djibouti Franc	DJF	262
DOMINICA	East Caribbean Dollar	XCD	951
DOMINICAN REPUBLIC	Dominican Peso	DOP	214
ECUADOR	US Dollar	USD	840
EGYPT	Egyptian Pound	EGP	818
EL SALVADOR	El Salvador Colon	SVC	USD
	US Dollar	222	840
ERITREA	Nakfa	ERN	232
ESTONIA	Kroon	EEK	233
ETHIOPIA	Ethiopian Birr	ETB	230
FALKLAND ISLANDS (MALVINAS)	Falkland Islands Pound	FKP	238
FAROE ISLANDS	Danish Krone	DKK	208
FIJI	Fiji Dollar	FJD	242
FINLAND	Euro	EUR	978
FRANCE	Euro	EUR	978
FRENCH GUIANA	Euro	EUR	978
FRENCH POLYNESIA	CFP Franc	XPF	953
FRENCH SOUTHERN TERRITORIES	Euro	EUR	978
GAMBIA	Dalasi	GMD	270
GEORGIA	Lari	GEL	981
GERMANY	Euro	EUR	978
GHANA	Cedi	GHC	288

GIBRALTAR	Gibraltar Pound	GIP	292
GREECE	Euro	EUR	978
GREENLAND	Danish Krone	DKK	208
GRENADA	East Caribbean Dollar	XCD	951
GUADELOUPE	Euro	EUR	978
GUAM	US Dollar	USD	840
GUATEMALA	Quetzal	GTQ	320
GUINEA	Guinea Franc	GNF	324
GUYANA	Guyana Dollar	GYD	328
HAITI	Gourde US Dollar	HTG 332	USD 840
HEARD ISLAND AND McDONALD ISLANDS	Australian Dollar	AUD	036
HOLY SEE (VATICAN CITY STATE)	Euro	EUR	978
HONDURAS	Lempira	HNL	340
HONG KONG	Hong Kong Dollar	HKD	344
HUNGARY	Forint	HUF	348
ICELAND	Iceland Krona	ISK	352
INDIA	Indian Rupee	INR	356
INDONESIA	Rupiah	IDR	360
INTERNATIONAL MONETARY FUND (I.M.F)	SDR	XDR	960
IRAN (ISLAMIC REPUBLIC OF)	Iranian Rial	IRR	364
IRAQ	Iraqi Dinar	IQD	368
IRELAND	Euro	EUR	978
ISRAEL	New Israeli Sheqel	ILS	376
ITALY	Euro	EUR	978
JAMAICA	Jamaican Dollar	JMD	388
JAPAN	Yen	JPY	392
JORDAN	Jordanian Dinar	JOD	400
KAZAKHSTAN	Tenge	KZT	398
KENYA	Kenyan Shilling	KES	404
KIRIBATI	Australian Dollar	AUD	036
KOREA, DEMOCRATIC PEOPLE'S REPUBLIC OF	North Korean Won	KPW	408
KOREA, REPUBLIC OF	Won	KRW	410
KUWAIT	Kuwaiti Dinar	KWD	414
KYRGYZSTAN	Som	KGS	417
LAO PEOPLE'S DEMOCRATIC REPUBLIC	Kip	LAK	418
LATVIA	Latvian Lats	LVL	428
LEBANON	Lebanese Pound	LBP	422
LESOTHO	Rand	ZAR	710

LESOTHO	Loti	LSL	426
LIBERIA	Liberian Dollar	LRD	430
LIBYAN ARAB JAMAHIRIYA	Libyan Dinar	LYD	434
LIECHTENSTEIN	Swiss Franc	CHF	756
LITHUANIA	Lithuanian Litas	LTL	440
LUXEMBOURG	Euro	EUR	978
MACAO	Pataca	MOP	446
MACEDONIA, THE FORMER YUGOSLAV REPUBLIC OF	Denar	MKD	807
MADAGASCAR	Malagascy Ariary	MGA	969
MALAWI	Kwacha	MWK	454
MALAYSIA	Malaysian Ringgit	MYR	458
MALDIVES	Rufiyaa	MVR	462
MALTA	Maltese Lira	MTL	470
MARSHALL ISLANDS	US Dollar	USD	840
MARTINIQUE	Euro	EUR	978
MAURITANIA	Ouguiya	MRO	478
MAURITIUS	Mauritius Rupee	MUR	480
MAYOTTE	Euro	EUR	978
MEXICO	Mexican Peso	MXN	484
	Mexican Unidad de Inversion (UID)	MXV	979
MICRONESIA (FEDERATED STATES OF)	US Dollar	USD	840
MOLDOVA, REPUBLIC OF	Moldovan Leu	MDL	498
MONACO	Euro	EUR	978
MONGOLIA	Tugrik	MNT	496
MONTENEGRO	Euro	EUR	978
MONTSERRAT	East Caribbean Dollar	XCD	951
MOROCCO	Moroccan Dirham	MAD	504
MOZAMBIQUE	Metical	MZN	943
MYANMAR	Kyat	MMK	104
NAMIBIA	Rand	ZAR	710
	Namibian Dollar	NAD	516
NAURU	Australian Dollar	AUD	036
NEPAL	Nepalese Rupee	NPR	524
NETHERLANDS	Euro	EUR	978
NETHERLANDS ANTILLES	Netherlands Antillian Guilder	ANG	532
NEW CALEDONIA	CFP Franc	XPF	953
NEW ZEALAND	New Zealand Dollar	NZD	554
NICARAGUA	Cordoba Oro	NIO	558
NIGERIA	Naira	NGN	566
NIUE	New Zealand Dollar	NZD	554
NORFOLK ISLAND	Australian Dollar	AUD	036

NORTHERN MARIANA ISLANDS	US Dollar	USD	840
NORWAY	Norwegian Krone	NOK	578
OMAN	Rial Omani	OMR	512
PAKISTAN	Pakistan Rupee	PKR	586
PALAU	US Dollar	USD	840
PANAMA	Balboa	PAB	590
	US Dollar	USD	840
PAPUA NEW GUINEA	Kina	PGK	598
PARAGUAY	Guarani	PYG	600
PERU	Nuevo Sol	PEN	604
PHILIPPINES	Philippine Peso	PHP	608
PITCAIRN	New Zealand Dollar	NZD	554
POLAND	Zloty	PLN	985
PORTUGAL	Euro	EUR	978
PUERTO RICO	US Dollar	USD	840
QATAR	Qatari Rial	QAR	634
RÉUNION	Euro	EUR	978
ROMANIA	Old Leu	ROL	642
	New Leu	RON	946
RUSSIAN FEDERATION	Russian Ruble	RUB	643
RWANDA	Rwanda Franc	RWF	646
SAINT HELENA	Saint Helena Pound	SHP	654
SAINT KITTS AND NEVIS	East Caribbean Dollar	XCD	951
SAINT LUCIA	East Caribbean Dollar	XCD	951
SAINT PIERRE AND MIQUELON	Euro	EUR	978
SAINT VINCENT AND THE GRENADINES	East Caribbean Dollar	XCD	951
SAMOA	Tala	WST	882
SAN MARINO	Euro	EUR	978
SÃO TOME AND PRINCIPE	Dobra	STD	678
SAUDI ARABIA	Saudi Riyal	SAR	682
SERBIA	Serbian Dinar	RSD	941
SEYCHELLES	Seychelles Rupee	SCR	690
SIERRA LEONE	Leone	SLL	694
SINGAPORE	Singapore Dollar	SGD	702
SLOVAKIA	Slovak Koruna	SKK	703
SLOVENIA	Tolar	SIT	705
SOLOMON ISLANDS	Solomon Islands Dollar	SBD	090
SOMALIA	Somali Shilling	SOS	706
SOUTH AFRICA	Rand	ZAR	710
SPAIN	Euro	EUR	978
SRI LANKA	Sri Lanka Rupee	LKR	144
SUDAN	Sudanese Dinar	SDG	938

SURINAME	Surinam Dollar	SRD	968
SVALBARD AND JAN MAYEN	Norwegian Krone	NOK	578
SWAZILAND	Lilangeni	SZL	748
SWEDEN	Swedish Krona	SEK	752
SWITZERLAND	Swiss Franc	CHF	756
	WIR Franc	CHW	948
	WIR Euro	CHE	947
SYRIAN ARAB REPUBLIC	Syrian Pound	SYP	760
TAIWAN, PROVINCE OF CHINA	New Taiwan Dollar	TWD	901
TAJIKISTAN	Somoni	TJS	972
TANZANIA, UNITED REPUBLIC OF	Tanzanian Shilling	TZS	834
THAILAND	Baht	THB	764
TIMOR-LESTE	US Dollar	USD	840
TOKELAU	New Zealand Dollar	NZD	554
TONGA	Pa'anga	TOP	776
TRINIDAD AND TOBAGO	Trinidad and Tobago Dollar	TTD	780
TUNISIA	Tunisian Dinar	TND	788
TURKEY	New Turkish Lira	TRY	949
TURKMENISTAN	Manat	TMM	795
TURKS AND CAICOS ISLANDS	US Dollar	USD	840
TUVALU	Australian Dollar	AUD	036
UGANDA	Uganda Shilling	UGX	800
UKRAINE	Hryvnia	UAH	980
UNITED ARAB EMIRATES	UAE Dirham	AED	784

UNITED KINGDOM	Pound Sterling	GBP	826
UNITED STATES	US Dollar	USD	840 998 997
UNITED STATES MINOR OUTLYING ISLANDS	US Dollar	USD	840
URUGUAY	Peso Uruguayo Uruguay Peso en Unidades Indexadas	UYU UYI	858 940
UZBEKISTAN	Uzbekistan Sum	UZS	860
VANUATU	Vatu	VUV	548
VENEZUELA	Bolivar	VEB	862
VIET NAM	Dong	VND	704
VIRGIN ISLANDS (BRITISH)	US Dollar	USD	840
VIRGIN ISLANDS (US)	US Dollar	USD	840
WALLIS AND FUTUNA	CFP Franc	XPF	953
WESTERN SAHARA	Moroccan Dirham	MAD	504
YEMEN	Yemeni Rial	YER	886
ZAMBIA	Kwacha	ZMK	894
ZIMBABWE	Zimbabwe Dollar	ZWD	716
Source: www.iso.org			

Major Regulatory Agencies

Australia

- Australian Securities and Investments Commission [www.asic.gov.au]

Canada

- Ontario Securities Commission [www.osc.gov.on.ca]
- British Columbia Securities Commission [www.bcsc.bc.ca]

Denmark

- The Danish Financial Supervisory Authority [www.dfsa.dk]

Hong Kong

- Securities and Futures Commission [www.sfc.hk]

Japan

- Financial Services Agency [www.fsa.go.jp]

Singapore

- Monetary Authority of Singapore [www.mas.gov.sg]

Switzerland

- Groupement Suisse des Conseils en Gestion Indépendants [www.gscgi.ch]
- Organisme d'autorégulation fondé par le GSCGI [www.oarg.ch]
- Association Romande des Intermediares Financiers [www.arif.ch]
- Swiss Federal Banking Commission [www.ebk.admin.ch]

United Kingdom

- Financial Services Authority [www.fsa.gov.uk]

United States

- Securities and Exchange Commission [www.sec.gov]

- National Futures Association [www.nfa.futures.org]

- Commodities and Futures Trading Commission [www.cftc.gov]

Index

Q